The 1857 Hamilton, Ontario Revival

McMaster Divinity College Press

McMaster General Series 6

The 1857 Hamilton, Ontario Revival

*An Exploration of the Origins of the Layman's Revival
and the Second Great Awakening*

by
SANDRA L. KING

PICKWICK *Publications* · Eugene, Oregon

THE 1857 HAMILTON, ONTARIO REVIVAL
An Exploration of the Origins of the Layman's Revival and the Second Great Awakening

McMaster Divinity College General Series 6

McMaster Divinity College
1280 Main Street West,
Hamilton, Ontario, Canada L8S 4K1

Pickwick Publications
An Imprint of Wipf and Stock Publishers
199 W. 8th Ave., Suite 3
Eugene, OR 97401

www.wipfandstock.com

ISBN 13: 978-1-4982-0946-5

Cataloguing-in-Publication Data

King, Sandra L.

The 1857 Hamilton, Ontario revival: an exploration of the origins of the Layman's Revival and the Second Great Awakening / Sandra L. King

xviii + 166 p. ; 23 cm. Includes bibliographical references and index..

1. Revival of 1857–1858. 2. Palmer, Phoebe. 3. Canada, Church History, 19th century. I. King, Sandra L. II. Title. III. Series

BV 3770.K 2015

Manufactured in the U.S.A.   08/12/2015

This book is dedicated
to the people of the city of
Hamilton, Ontario.

God knows you, has seen your heart,
understands what has happened,
and has not forgotten you.

Contents

Illustrations

1867 Map of Canada West. By Augustus Mitchell, Jr., Antique Maps & Works on Paper Ltd. Used with Permission from David and Natasha Deighton. www.mapsandart.com.   13

Bird's Eye View Map of Hamilton. Published by Rice & Duncan 1859. Image courtesy of Hamilton Public Library, Local History and Archives.   14

The Gore, ca. 1860–63. The water fountain seen here was installed after the revival for the visit of the Prince of Wales in 1860. Image courtesy of Hamilton Public Library, Local History and Archives. Mills Family Album.   15

Desjardins Canal Accident Lithograph. By H. Gregory, from an Ambrotype by O. N. Preston. March 12, 1857, Courtesy of Public Archives, Canada. Image courtesy of Hamilton Public Library, Local History and Archives. Desjardins Canal Accident Lithograph.   19

Map of Hamilton showing location of the three churches participating in the revival. The map is clearly constructed shortly after the revival, as it indicates the location of the Wesleyan Female College that was established or perhaps under construction at the time. "City of Hamilton: Scale 12 Chains to One Inch." Map. Montreal, QC: Burland Desbarats Lith., ca. 1858–60. Donated to Hamilton Public Library, Local History and Archives, by Charles Hogg in 2001. Image courtesy of Hamilton Public Library, Local History and Archives.   37

Zion Methodist Church. Personal collection, 2007.   40

Acknowledgements

S PECIAL THANKS GO TO the following:

- To Ken Bosveld, who gave me this assignment for the *Beacon* magazine to cultivate my research and writing skills. You have been a source of encouragement to write the story.

- To Bruce Woods for initially writing locally about the 1857 Hamilton Revival and sharing it with those who wanted to see God move again. Your generosity in sharing where to get some of the original documentation for the research has made this possible.

- To Paul Fayter for your knowledge of historical research, what archives to access (including the ones at First-Pilgrim United Church), initial copyediting of the main body of this work, and your encouragement to be as accurate as possible. you have been a blessing to me in the duration of this project.

- To Mary DeGeer, who helped copyedit my Literature Review (chapter 1), Methodist Revivals, and the Uniqueness of the Hamilton Revival (chapter 3), along with a few other sections. Your grace and wisdom helped me to navigate the literature review and to keep the main points of the research in the forefront.

- To the Archives at McMaster Divinity College and the Periodical collection at Mills Library, McMaster University, the Hamilton Public Library, and York University. The staff at all these locations worked to help me achieve accuracy and unearth hidden facts about the Revival. I could not have done it without you.

- To Gordon Heath, for seeing the potential and value of my manuscript. Thank you for helping me understand the steps I needed to take to get my manuscript to a reasonable level of academic competence.

- To Lois Dow at McMaster Divinity College Press for your editing skills that kept the storyline flowing, accurate, and grammatically correct. Your improvements and eye for accuracy have not only made this book better, but have enabled it to reach a higher level of academic value. I believe that everyone needs a good editor like you.

- To the pastors of Hamilton, whose love and devotion to the city kept encouraging me to dig deeper for this story. We all want God to pour out His Spirit in this amazing history-changing city in a big way again. Let's keep praying!

ABOUT THE AUTHOR

Sandra King grew up and lives in the Hamilton area. She studied at Elim Bible Institute in Lima, New York. After graduating she did street ministry in downtown Hamilton, and completed five missionary trips.

Sandra also has a post-graduate education in Public Relations from Niagara College. It was during these studies that she discovered her ability to write. Upon graduation she held several free-lance writing jobs, one for a Christian regional magazine called *Beacon*. Her editor assigned her to write an article for the 150th Anniversary of the Revival. That was when she began to seriously research what actually happened in Hamilton in 1857.

Sandra is passionate about Hamilton, ministry, history, and people.

Introduction

PERSONALLY, I LOVE STUDYING the 1857 Revival in Hamilton. It reminds me as a Christian that history is a demonstration to people of faith that God is powerful and can do incredible things despite our shortcomings. We can study these times to remind ourselves that God moved once, and he can do it again. My only caution is that we do not look for God to move in the same way as he did in the past. God only parted the Red Sea once (Exodus 13–14), there is only one Savior who was nailed to the cross for all of time (Matthew 27, Mark 15, Luke 23, John 19), and the tongues of fire that settled above the disciples' heads at Pentecost came only once (Acts 2). God is always doing something new; we need to keep our eyes, minds, and hearts open to his next move. I do believe that God will come in a mighty move once again over Hamilton. It is important to know spiritual history, but also to watch for the new way in which God comes, so that we don't miss his moving.

Although this research does not answer every question, I believe you will find it a blessing that will minister to your spirit. As we peer through the annals of history, I trust you will see people you can relate to and find a story that gives hope. I know I did. It was comforting to know that the church of the past struggled with the same issues that the modern day church does, but they pressed on to prevail. It was also a comfort to see how the key figures came through challenges of their own in their personal lives (deaths and losses) and in their external lives (trains and schedules), but more importantly, how they used those circumstances to press on toward God.

One of the most powerful things that struck me while doing this research was the kind of people God used and the city God chose to bring about this event. Phoebe Palmer, a woman who had struggles, but was ahead of her time in giving and evangelizing—and dare I say it— preaching as a female (despite the fact that she was not given the formal role of a preacher), was used tremendously in this movement. She cared about the oppressed. Hamilton also has a history of loving those who are in need and in chains. Her husband Walter, who came with her, was a doctor, and he came to Hamilton, a city that has long had medical DNA in its history. I find it amazing that the heart of this city was reflected in the very woman (and couple) who brought a message of hope, a call to duty, and a change of heart that went worldwide.

Hamilton has long been an innovative community, one that birthed the Catholic School system, and was the home of Egerton Ryerson, a scholar and preacher who would bring the public school system into existence. Hamilton was also the home of significant politicians (Lester Bowles Pearson, Prime Minister of Canada) and mediators (Rev. Peter Jones a.k.a. Kahkewaquonaby of the Mississauga North American Indians). It has been the birthplace of innovative ideas that have changed the world, such as the creation of the first iron steamboat to sail in fresh water in North America, the first electric streetcars (and for a long while with the longest length of rail), the first telephone exchange in the British Empire, and the first long distance hydroelectric power transmission in the world. There the first sulphur matches were invented and produced (interesting to note that God would "spark" a revival from Hamilton). From Hamilton came the first goalie pads, Tim Horton's, and Lifesavers candy. Hamilton has produced leaders in the steel industry, scientific innovation, and the medical sector.[1] The city has had a profound, but little-known effect on the world.

The 1857 Hamilton Revival is known by several names. First, it has been called the Layman's Revival, because it was started and carried out by laymen.[2] The word "layman" means a non-ordained person, non-clergy, or one who has not taken formal theological training. During the Hamilton Revival people were converting to Christianity via a move among the laymen.

Second, it was part of a movement informally called by some the Shopkeepers' Revival. A few days after the Hamilton Revival was in full swing, word of this move of God spread to New York. In New York City, a group of businessmen were closing up shop to attend noon-hour prayer meetings that later became known as the Fulton Street Prayer meetings. Most likely they were seeking God because their country was facing seri-

1. Watson and MacDonald, *History of Hamilton and District*, chs. 20 and 25.
2. Towns and Porter, *Ten Greatest Revivals Ever*, ch. 5.

ous issues such as civil war and financial crisis. Although these meetings were gaining in popularity, after the Bank Panic was declared official (and not just temporary) there was dramatic increase in attendance at these meetings. Thus the Shopkeepers' Revival was born. These prayer meetings were so packed that people were hanging off every available space just to be a part of what God was doing.

Lastly it was known as an Awakening because those who participated became alive spiritually once again, moving from a place where church was the right thing to do, to a place where God was alive in their life. They spread this passion and good news to others, thus in a sense awakening the worldwide church from its slumber.[3] The 1857 Hamilton Revival is usually considered to be part of the Second Great Awakening.

The Second Great Awakening cannot be tied up into one simple package. It is more like a tangled bush with off-shoots all over the place. As Kathryn Long says, "The word 'awakening' usually was reserved for . . . a prolonged revival movement, although on occasion it, too, was employed in the more narrow sense."[4] Therefore, I have done my best to capture the root of the revival that started in Canada, while including some of the off-shoots.

The Second Great Awakening became a collection of many revivals worldwide. It continued for at least seven or eight years (or more, depending on how you trace the effects), but as with every revival, it is easier to document a start than the finish. In revivals there will always be stronger events that trigger other events and create movements, churches, and organizations. There will also be events that last for a short while and do not trigger other events or the building of something new.

I would like to note at this point that prior to research for this book, I had read a few books about the Great Awakening, one being Bruce L. Shelly's, *Church History in Plain Language*. Shelly categorized this movement as the Third Great Awakening, considering the First Great Awakening as occurring about 1720–40 (the movement in which John Wesley came to warm and more personally confident faith). The second, according to Shelly, was between 1790 and 1800 in the regions between the Alleghenies and the Mississippi, while the movement that included the Hamilton Revival was the third.[5] I based some of my previous writ-

---

3. Orr and Roberts, *Event of the Century*, 23–38.

4. Long, *Revival of 1857–58*, 9.

5. Shelley, *Church History in Plain Language*, 406–7.

ings on Shelly's classification, calling the 1857 Hamilton Revival part of the Third Great Awakening. Since then, I have studied more historians who maintain that this was part of the Second Great Awakening. They see the 1790 revival as a smaller event that did not stretch as far as the first and later ones did. I have now come to agree with the majority of other historians. The bottom line is this: there was a revival in Hamilton in 1857 that became part of a great awakening. Whether we call it the second or the third awakening is not as important as the fact that it happened. I apologize for any confusion this may cause for those who have studied my previous work and who may be confused by my periodization of this.

May you be blessed as you read about Hamilton's past foundations and look forward to the future. May Hamilton's story resonate in your heart, move you to prayer, and help you to be all that God created you to be.

1

1857 Hamilton Revival Historical Sources

I FIRST LEARNED ABOUT this revival through a Hamilton pastor, Bruce Woods. He had written a small informal paper on it and circulated it among the area pastors. It was an exciting paper that had a few gaps in it, but the local Christians loved this little piece of history.

Fast forward to 2006, and I was writing for a Christian magazine called the *Beacon.* The editor had assigned me and another writer to cover the 1857 Revival but from different perspectives. I was specifically assigned to investigate the origins of the original churches involved. This research led me to Paul Fayter who, at the time, was the minister at First-Pilgrim United Church. This church's heritage comes from one of the original churches in the revival. Fortunately, Paul was also a historian interested especially in Canadian history during that time period. He began to help me piece together a clearer and deeper understanding of this story. As I said in the introduction, my research and magazine article originally concluded that the 1857 Hamilton Revival was a part of the Third Great Awakening, but my later research uncovered stronger evidence that the Hamilton Revival was more likely to have been part of the Second Great Awakening.

After the initial magazine article was published and during subsequent speaking engagements about my findings, I found avid interest and more questions (from myself and others) regarding this aspect of local church history. I had discovered during my initial research that few historians even mentioned the fact that Hamilton had a revival in 1857, and when they did speak of it, they only provided brief overviews, with conflicting opinions as to the facts of the event. So, in light of the local interest shown and a desire for a more comprehensive historical account about the event, I decided to dig deeper and turn my years of research into this book. The goal of this volume is to establish, to the best of my ability, what major events occurring in 1857 affected Hamilton, what churches were involved, the key players, the unique features of the revival, how it unfolded, how it was a significant part of the Second Great Awakening, and, finally, what happened after the revival. Hopefully, I will be able to equip readers with enough historical evidence to provide a good foundation for understanding this amazing move of God.

In order to keep the power of the storyline of the Hamilton revival flowing in the account in the next chapters, I have chosen to discuss some of the differences in historical documentation and interpretations of other authors in this section and in the background sections for the reader to reference.

There is limited primary source documentation crediting Hamilton as the start of this revival or even as being a part of the Great Awakening. However, Phoebe Palmer, an instrumental key leader, wrote about her experiences and reflections during the revival in her journals and other various publications, and her eyewitness account gives legitimacy to the story. The main sources for the account are Phoebe's writings, articles in the American Methodist paper the *Christian Advocate and Journal* for 1857 and 1858, and the Canadian Methodist newspaper *The Christian Guardian*. The two main books containing many of Phoebe's letters about the revival are Phoebe Palmer's *Promise of the Father* and Richard Wheatley's *The Life and Letters of Phoebe Palmer*. The latter book was published initially by a family member, and later by others, including Richard Wheatley, who preached with Walter and Phoebe Palmer and with Catherine and William Booth (who co-founded the Salvation Army). Wheatley published Phoebe Palmer's work and letters in 1867 under the title *Annus Mirabilis*, which means "year of wonders."

Notes on Phoebe and Walter Palmer, and some of Phoebe's letters, are also referenced from Thomas C. Oden's book *Phoebe Palmer: Selected Writings*, Harold E. Raser's book *Phoebe Palmer: Her Life and Thought*, and Charles White's *The Beauty of Holiness: Phoebe Palmer as Theologian*. These books are good resources, but I found that some of their information did not match the primary source documents. In all fairness though, the Hamilton Revival was not their main thrust, and the other information was useful and credible in understanding Phoebe's life with insights into her friendships, colleagues, and affiliations.

J. Edwin Orr's extensive writings about this period were an invaluable resource. Mr. Orr (1912–84) was born in Ireland and worked as a Chaplain in the US Air Force. His mother, as well, grew up in Ireland, near where the first Irish revivals took place. She was touched by the stories of this revival (or Awakening) and led Edwin to Christ. Inspired by this, Orr did research on this Awakening, which included the Hamilton Revival, and wrote a popular book titled *The Second Evangelical Awakening*, and an academic book, *The Event of the Century: The 1857–1859 Awakening*. Although some of his information is not accurate (some errors may be due to the latter book being a posthumous publication), it was a solid guide and overview.

Peter George Bush wrote a Master's thesis on the Hamilton Revival at Queen's University in 1985. I mainly concentrated on chapters 1 and 2, and read parts of chapters 3, 5, and 6. Bush's thesis was mainly to demonstrate that, despite some people's opinion, revivals still occurred in the 1850s. Bush outlined the travels of James Caughey and the Palmers. He provided some solid research into the Hamilton Revival, but missed some of Phoebe Palmer's important letters, and had a few minor errors in his research, most likely due to how he read and handled the material (similarly to Orr). An example is the following quotation: "Dr. Palmer went to see if he and his wife could make connections for New York City that night and discovered that they could not. He checked their baggage through to Albany on the morning train; then he and his wife took their overnight bags and headed for the house of a friend near the Hamilton train station."[1] My research shows that the Palmers arrived by train in Hamilton, and were for some reason unable to check their baggage to board the boat to Albany New York, thus creating a delay. A minor adjustment is needed to see the real picture as to what happened that night. A reading of Phoebe Palmer's writings will demonstrate this. I believe that in some matters, such as in this account, the author was reading between the lines, using his own interpretation as to what may have occurred. Since this event was not the key focus of Bush's writing, some speculative interpretation is understandable, whereas my book specifically delves deeper into the details of the revival, and therefore requires a deeper level of accuracy on the finer points. However, a majority of Bush's and my research overlapped and aligned. This was especially

---

1. Bush, "James Caughey, Phoebe and Walter Palmer," 1. Orr, *Event of the Century*, 26, also states that the Palmers' baggage went astray, but again that was not the case.

confirming since Bush's thesis was a late discovery, after a major part of my work had been completed.

Timothy Smith's book *Revivalism and Social Reform in Mid-Nineteenth Century America* has a section that reports the occurrence of the Hamilton Revival in 1857 and gives a broad overview, but it is not totally accurate regarding the number of new coverts. I believe he read some of Phoebe's letters, but did not realize that the numbers increased as more reports came in. In her October 14th letter to her sister Sarah Lankford, Phoebe mentioned that ten days into the revival there were 400 saved, but at the end she stated that she had just been informed that the true number was 500.[2] I also believed he missed Samuel Rice's letters that document 600 converts in Hamilton as more came to Christ after the Palmers left. Smith does, however, recognize the Hamilton Revival as a significant contribution to the beginning of the larger 1857–58 Great Awakening. He explains how the Hamilton Revival fits into the movement, its uniqueness because it was not just that individuals were converted but that the churches began to become spiritually alive again, as well as this revival's significance for the beginning of the Great Awakening.

> Nor were protracted meetings in rural and small-town churches unimportant. William C. Conant's compilation reveals that 88 towns in Maine, 40 in New Hampshire, 39 in Vermont and 147 in Massachusetts experienced unusual awakenings. Some of these, to be sure, may have been quite ordinary meetings which persons caught up in the universal excitement glowingly reported. But other evidence abounds. Methodists Walter and Phoebe Palmer wrote of conversions by the hundreds and crowds of 5,000–6,000 at obscure camp meetings in Ontario and Quebec in 1857. That fall an afternoon prayer meeting in Hamilton, Ontario, stretched into a ten day's revival in which 400 were converted and scores sanctified. Lay testimonies rather than sermons, particularly in the afternoon meetings for holiness, were, Mrs. Palmer believed, chiefly responsible for these results.[3]

Smith also had a good grasp of the struggle that the Methodists had regarding the entire sanctification that was popularized by evangelists such as Phoebe Palmer. His research was helpful in explaining

---

2. Wheatley, *Life and Letters of Mrs. Phoebe Palmer*, 330–32.

3. Smith, *Revivalism and Social Reform*, 67.

the thoughts of both the Methodist Church leaders and Phoebe Palmer on the subject.

In comparison, Kathryn Long, in her book *Revival of 1857–58: Interpreting an American Religious Awakening*, gets the information for her overview right and acknowledges the Hamilton Revival as part of the Great Awakening. However, she does not feel it played a significant part as a catalyst for the larger movement. She credits the awakening as being started in New York by Jeremiah Lanphier. In the quote below, Long's examination of the first pastors, church historians, and American newspapers that recorded the awakening indicates her thoughts on the origin.

> What was the initial picture that emerged from their books? First, there was a basic consensus about the origin of the revival. It was a supernatural movement of God that began, appropriately enough, in an "upper room," a third-floor classroom in a building that formed part of the North Dutch Church at the corner of William and Fulton Streets in downtown New York City.[4]

In the third chapter of her book, she further states: "The October 1857 experience of Phoebe and Walter Palmer in Hamilton, Ontario, [was] one of the earliest recognized expressions of revival."[5] Although she calls this an "expression of revival," she still does not count it as the beginning of an awakening. She does say however, that "during autumn 1857, scattered local revivals appeared, encouraged by the social context of church and family, especially in the wake of financial panic. There was little indication, however, that these were unusually widespread or part of a broader trend until late December and early January."[6] In fact, in her Appendix A, Long skips over documentation of the success that the Palmers had in Ontario that summer, culminating with the significant revival in Hamilton. Long's research and understanding of the American newspaper articles written during the Second Great Awakening is excellent and helpful, but does not seem to dig into enough other primary source accounts to broaden her perspective. To me, this, along with her differentiation between the terms "revival" and "awakening," clearly influenced her stance that New York was the start of the Great Awakening.

4. Long, *Revival of 1857–58*, 13.
5. Ibid., 49.
6. Ibid., 60.

Lastly, Richard Carwardine's book *Trans-Atlantic Revivalism: Popular Evangelism in Britain and America* loosely attributes the beginnings of the Awakening to Hamilton.

> By 1857 the Palmers had become celebrities whose sense of their own centrality in a widening revival movement was heightened when in October in Hamilton, Canada West [Ontario], they presided over a revival regarded by some contemporaries as causally connected with the seminal New York movement of that year.[7]

Phyllis Airhart, another Canadian Methodist expert, did not write about the Hamilton Revival, but was extremely helpful for understanding Wesleyan Methodist theology, especially around revivals. Two rich resources I used to understand Canadian Methodism in the nineteenth century were Neil Semple's *The Lord's Dominion: The History of Canadian Methodism* (chapters 1–3, 6, 9) and William Westfall's *Two Worlds: The Protestant Culture of Nineteenth Century Ontario* (mainly the first three chapters). Semple briefly mentions that there was a revival in Hamilton. Although Westfall does not speak about the Hamilton 1857 Revival, he provides an understanding of how Canadian Methodist revivals were viewed. I also utilized Marilyn Färdig Whiteley's book *Canadian Methodist Women, 1766–1925: Marys, Marthas, Mothers in Israel*, chapter 4, to shed some light on the role of women in the Canadian Methodist Church.

As well as accessing the local Hamilton archives and libraries, churches, McMaster University (including the archives at McMaster Divinity College), and the Methodist archives (now United Church archives), I used a variety of materials to understand the background concerning the key players and the churches most involved in the revival.

To research the key personalities in the revival, I was able to obtain information through several volumes of the *Dictionary of Hamilton Biography*, the *Christian Herald* magazine, the periodical *Methodist History*, the Methodist newspapers, and various credible websites. I also happened to come across a reference to a Mrs. Boice who was present during the revival. There were a few lines about the Hamilton Revival in her obituary in the *Christian Guardian*. Although the information clearly pointed to the 1857 revival in Hamilton, the date was wrong.

---

7. Carwardine, *Transatlantic Revivalism*, 182.

To research the churches involved, I relied on period maps of Hamilton, as well as Ralph Pawson's *Growing Together: A History of First-Pilgrim United Church, Hamilton, Ontario*, which gave a strong historical background and starting point for the Methodist (now United) Churches in Hamilton. After reading the book, I was able to access First-Pilgrim United Church's archives (a church whose origins come from First Church), and Centenary United Church's history (a church built after the revival). This proved to be a bit of a challenge, as at times there were some inaccuracies in the information written in many pamphlets or flyers. By comparing the resources with the information I knew to be accurate, I was able to fill in the pieces of the puzzle. This required a lot of time and effort. The remainder of the information was accessed through the United Church Archives, using the Wesleyan Methodist Circuit Records, Vol. XIV, and "Wesley United Church (Hamilton, Ont.) fonds," as well as a few Hamilton newspapers.

To understand what the other denominations in Hamilton felt about the revival, I searched for information on that period, using maps and making notes as to what churches were around during that period, and uncovering which churches hosted the revival. I was able to access the *Canada Christian Advocate*, a Methodist Church newspaper, containing an article during the revival's time, treating "Why There Is No More Revival." Furthermore, when I asked local church historians from other denominations that were present during the time, they did not have any documents on their churches' participation in the revival. However, in the body of my work you will discover a letter from Reverend Samuel Rice that states that there were other churches in the city involved in the revival (see ch. 6 p. 79). In light of these findings it seems that if there were other denominations involved besides the Wesleyans/Methodists, there is no documentation of it that has been uncovered thus far. It was after I had done this legwork that I read Bush's thesis to discover he had met with the same conclusion about the churches, but it appears that I may have done a bit more extensive work then he.

To understand the setting of Hamilton in 1857, I accessed the *Census of the Canadas*, the *1858 City of Hamilton Directory*, (with information that was compiled in 1857; there is no directory for 1857), maps of Hamilton, John C. Weavers's book *Hamilton: An Illustrated History*, Milton Watson and Charles MacDonald's book *The History of Hamilton and District*, and the Hamilton Public Library Local Archives, in which

I accessed pictures and articles on the time period. J. Edwin Orr's book provided material on what was occurring in the world during that period. I was able to obtain additional information through interviewing Paul Fayter, a Hamilton historian who specializes in the Victorian era, and from materials on the internet.

To understand what happened during the Great Awakening after it left Hamilton I used Phoebe Palmer's writings, J. Edwin Orr's material, Elmer L. Towns and Douglas Porter's book *The Ten Greatest Revivals Ever: From Pentecost to the Present*, as well as *The New York Times*, and works from the internet. As a side note: Towns and Porter are scholars who analyze revivals. They state that their work is documented, but not in the normal scholarly manner, as it is meant "to touch hearts of readers and to challenge them to revival."[8] Having reviewed a majority of their sources for information, and piecing together what they have written, I believe it to be accurate, so I continued to use their information in the body of my work. A great resource that I used in understanding what occurred in New York at the Fulton Street prayer meetings was the book *Power of Prayer: Illustrated in the Wonderful Displays of Divine Grace at the Fulton Street and Other Meetings in New York and Elsewhere in 1857 and 1858*, by Samuel Irenaeus Prime. This was informative, as it carried excerpts from Jeremiah Lanphier's diary (the man who headed the prayer meetings). He does note that the prayer meetings might have been affected by the Bank Panic, but believes it was more of a divine move of God.

To enhance the section on D. L. Moody, I used his son's work titled *The Life of Dwight L. Moody*, which was written to clarify misunderstandings about his father, and was printed on D. L. Moody's brother-in-law's press in 1900. I also obtained information from *The Life and Work of D. L. Moody* written by Rev. Chapman who was a close friend of Mr. Moody for 20 years. Lastly, I accessed Moody's book *To the Work! To the Work! Exhortations to Christians* in order to document a quotation that I felt reflected the heart of the revival. The quotation has been used by many, but not documented properly.

There were two references that I used to understand the story of Joseph Scriven. The first was from the *Dictionary of Canadian Biography* and the second was *What a Friend We Have in Jesus: And Other Hymns by Joseph Scriven* written by a Canadian minister, Rev. James Cleland,

8. Towns and Porter, *Ten Greatest Revivals Ever*, Introduction.

to honor Scriven's passing. These along with other documents from the internet were very useful.

To research the history of the Song *Jesus Loves Me*, the book *Say and Seal, Vol. II* was accessed to see the original poem by Anna Bartlett Warner. The music used when the poem was turned into a song is documented in William Bradbury's *New Golden Trio: "New Golden Chain," "New Golden Shower" and "New Golden Censer."* Although I would have liked to uncover more about William Bradbury's thoughts on why he chose to turn the poem into a song, I was unable to resource this information.

When the Great Awakening continued on in Hamilton's backyard (Grimsby), I turned to the Grimsby archives and used Harriet Phelps Younan's book *Grimsby Park Historical and Geographical Sketches* to understand the events surrounding the campground.

Although this research is laden with good information, there is always more digging to be done, more questions to research. To help the research on the revival, it would have been nice to have had other resources listed below.

1. It would have been useful to have more contemporary local religious newspapers for their coverage of the revival, whether from the Hamilton Methodists or from other denominations.

2. Though this revival seems to be a significant event in Canadian religious history, after an extensive search I found no *Hamilton Spectator* coverage of this revival.

3. In doing due diligence to authors who had written a little bit about the Hamilton Revival, I looked for three primary sources mentioned. The first, was listed by Orr (p. 27 in *The Event of the Century*) as the *Centennial Souvenir of First Methodist Church, Hamilton, Ontario, Canada 1821–1924*, with information stating that the Hamilton mayor had given testimony during a revival meeting by which people were warmed. Having looked through this primary source, I discovered the mayor's name and family business, but nothing about a testimony as the documentation suggested. Likewise, Orr mentioned an article "Revival Messenger" in *The Christian Advocate and Journal*, June 3, 1858, that does not seem to be in that issue. The other reference came from Bush, who noted a primary source document about the revival in *The Guardian* dated November 10, 1857 (p. 136 of his work). Again, I located the primary source but was unable to locate the document. I looked at

varying dates in November to try and source this article, but to no avail. I would have liked to have seen these three primary accounts, but believe somehow the documentation was mislabeled.

4. I was unable to locate any notes on who the other ministers might have been that came to the revival, what their denominations or affiliations were, and their thoughts and reflections on the event.

5. I was not able to gather a good variety of participants' accounts of the revival, so I am left to wonder what the thoughts of those attending were, as well as what specifically happened afterwards to those participating.

These are a few of the things that, if accessible, would fill in the gaps in this research. Please enjoy my research on the Hamilton 1857 Revival. May you be taken back by the uniqueness and the blessing of this event, as I have been.

Note: All italics and parenthesis in primary source quotations are from the original published text. The only exception is with the use of square brackets, which indicates words added to make the quotation read properly within the larger sentence. As well, square brackets are used in the Appendix to indicate differences between two published versions of Phoebe Palmer's letter to Rev. W.H.D.

2

Setting the Stage: 1857

WORLDWIDE

1857 was both a challenging year and a year of blessings. As good as the previous few years had been, the economic tides were starting to turn worldwide. Nevertheless, the advancement of modern technology was beginning to make the world a smaller place for news and travel. In the year 1857, communications were often delivered by word of mouth, newspapers, or letters. Travel was still common by foot and by horse, and long journeys across the ocean from Europe to North America were taken by boarding ships powered by sails (thirty days or more) or steam (fifteen days or less).[1] In Canada and the United States the railways were just extending their reach into settled regions and cities and would soon help to expedite the process of both travel and communication. The fairly new invention of the telegraph was being used by the railway companies for communication. The year following the start of the Hamilton revival, in 1858, Queen Victoria sent the first transatlantic cable message to US President Buchanan, opening a whole new opportunity to connect the old and new worlds together. Europe was starting to recover from the Crimean war (1853–56), meaning that Europe had less dependence on the new world for resources. The Irish potato famine had tragic and far reaching effects.[2]

1. "Information Sheet," Merseyside Maritime Museum, Liverpool, England. Online: http://www.liverpoolmuseums.org.uk/maritime/archive/sheet/64. See also J.-P. Rodrigue, "The Geography of Transport Systems." Online: https://people.hofstra.edu/geotrans/eng/ch3en/conc3en/linertransatlantic.html.

2. Orr and Roberts, *Event of the Century*, 3.

In the southern United States, slavery was still an issue that tore apart congregations, denominations, and a nation. The collapse of a major US bank in August, and subsequent failure of many businesses, by mid-October brought about the Great Bank Panic of 1857, leaving many unemployed and on the streets.[3] The California gold rush was coming to an end. It was the beginning of an international depression.[4]

According to J. Edwin Orr, in 1857 the churches worldwide were waning in number as people had put the love of money before the love of God. To further people's mistrust, the churches had been preaching the nearness of Christ's second coming to motivate people to repent for so long that many had become skeptical and ridiculed the church. This impaired public faith in religion. Orr sums it up by saying, "The zeal of people was devoted to the accumulation of wealth, and other things, including religion, took a lesser place. Boom times caught the public fancy, and turned men's hearts from God."[5]

Nathan O. Hatch, a professor of history at the University of Notre Dame, recounts that the region from Canada West (especially near Lake Ontario) to New York was called the Burned Over District: "The fires of the Spirit revived many lives there. But the expression also points to the many people who had high religious emotion that didn't stick, leaving them spiritually burnt out."[6]

3. Ibid.

4. Henley, interview.

5. Orr, *Second Evangelical Awakening*, 7.

6. "Revivals that Changed a Nation," 44.

CANADA

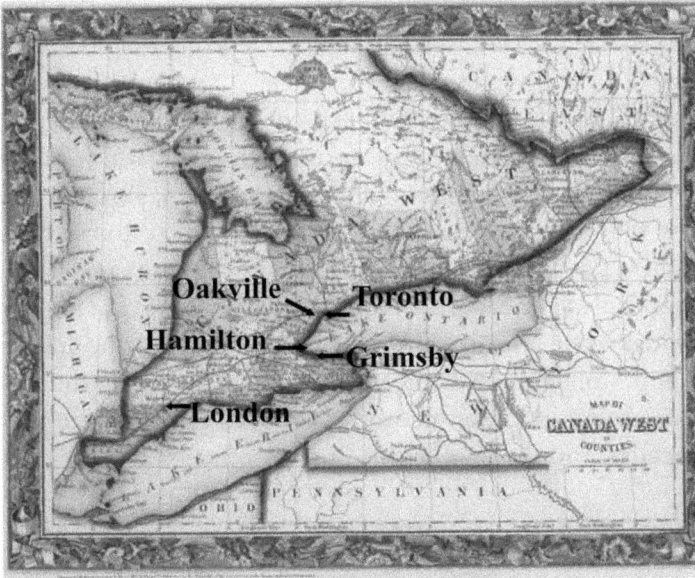

1867 Map of Canada West

Canada was not a formal nation in 1857, but was called the Province of Canada, administered by a responsible government as part of British North America. Canada was not officially formed as a nation until confederation in 1867, ten years later.

In 1857, Canada was divided into two parts: Canada East (formerly known as Lower Canada), and Canada West (formerly known as Upper Canada). The Atlantic provinces of Nova Scotia, New Brunswick, Prince Edward Island, and Newfoundland and Labrador were separate provinces or colonies with their own governments, collectively known as British North America, part of the British Empire.

Canada East was comprised of the southern part of what we know today as the province of Quebec. Canada West's borders were roughly those of what we know as southern Ontario today. The remainder of Canada had not been settled or explored by people of European descent much beyond this point. Hamilton, where our story begins, was situated in Canada West.

In 1857, streets were mud paths, and many still lived in log houses, although stone, brick, and clapboard structures were on the rise. In the

1830s and 40s major roadways were being cleared, charted, and used. Canal builders had finished most of their major construction. Roads and canals made transportation between communities and cities faster and more accessible.[7] It was a busy time for the expanding and emerging Canada.

The expanding railways by 1855 connected the United States to Canada, and what we know as the near north in Ontario (Collingwood and Georgian Bay) to Southern Ontario (Hamilton, Toronto, Niagara). The new railway connection brought a peak year of tourism and immigration (32,000 immigrants) to Canada in 1857. The railway brought not only people to Canada, but industry, wealth, news, and a connection to the wider world (via mail and newspapers). By 1859, the link between Sarnia and Montreal was complete, aiding once again in the spread of travel and communication networks, connecting what were known as "the Canadas" together even more.

HAMILTON

Bird's Eye View Map of Hamilton

---

7. Fayter, interview.

The Gore, ca. 1860–63.

Hamilton in 1857 was situated in Canada West at the head of Lake Ontario, and was a growing community. The population of Hamilton in 1856 was 21,855 and by 1858 it had grown to 27,500.[8] Hamilton's population was still smaller than Toronto's, but the city was just as important, and it was contending with Toronto for significance in Canada.

The official borders of the City of Hamilton in 1857 started just above Markland Street at the base of the escarpment, (the Hamilton section of the Niagara escarpment is referred to today as the "Hamilton Mountain") ending at the lake, and stretched westward slightly past Dundurn Street, and as far east as Wentworth Street. The community atop the "Hamilton Mountain" was known as the township of Barton. In 1960 the City of Hamilton annexed the township of Barton, and extended the city's borders by doing so.[9]

Between 1850 and 1860, Hamilton's settlers consisted of large numbers of people from the British Isles, and Persians, as well as a population of what was listed in *the Census of the Canadas* as "coloured." In smaller numbers were those from Italy and Greece, Spain and Portugal, Sweden and Norway, Russia and Poland, East India, and Germany, as well as native French and North American First Nations. There was also a list-

8. *City of Hamilton Population.*
9. *City of Hamilton History.*

ing for those who did not know their origins, or did not or could not communicate them.[10] Hamilton, even in its early years, already had the makings of a multicultural city.

During 1857 there were a lot of mainline churches in Hamilton, including United Empire Loyalist Methodist churches (that started in the 1790s), Baptist, Presbyterian, and Anglican.[11] If you have the opportunity, take a look at two Hamilton structures that were around in 1857 so that you can get a feel for the times and the architecture. The first is Christ's Church (Anglican) Cathedral on James Street North that officially opened the main stone structure in 1855. After the main structure was opened, the church continued to expand its building with detailed craftsmanship over many years.[12] The second is St. Paul's Presbyterian (originally St. Andrew's) on James Street South, kitty-corner to the YMCA. The finishing touches were put on the building in 1857 (the very year the revival took place). It is an ornate church that has managed to preserve many of its historic features.[13] The masonry, details, and large size of these two buildings are absolutely astounding, giving insight into the times. I encourage you to take a look if you can, inside these churches.

The Good Times in Hamilton

The years 1850–57 proved to be a time of economic growth, development, and prosperity for Hamilton, as it was a sophisticated cosmopolitan city for its time.[14] The city boasted the Mechanics Institute (the forerunner to the library), hotels, a brewery, a post-office, an orphanage, a handful of colleges, an ironworks business, a curling club, one of the two saw manufacturing companies in Canada, a manufacturer of ready-made clothes, and a rare sight—a sewing machine factory. Interestingly enough, Hamilton's public circulating newspaper was called *The Spectator*, as it still is today.

---

10. *Census of the Canadas 1851–1852. Personal Census*, 35 See also *Census of the Canadas 1860–1861*, 49.

11. Shephard, *1858 City of Hamilton Directory*, 22–23.

12. *Pilgrim's Guide to Christ's Church Cathedral*, 1–2, 11. See also *Welcome to Christ's Church*.

13. Bellamy and Riley, *St. Paul's Church*.

14. Henley, interview.

The waterfront had a steady barge industry with growing leisure activities such as yachting races and summer and winter festivities. Many sports, including baseball (a modern game imported from the United States) were played in the city. Civil engineers, confectioners, brokers, Indian herb doctors, dentists, as well as physicians and surgeons brought their practices to the city to establish them, and called Hamilton their home.[15]

The *1858 City of Hamilton Directory* could easily have doubled as a tourist guide attracting visitors and settlers to Hamilton. The following is a great description of Hamilton's desirable setting that was drawing people to the city:

> Few cities furnish to men of wealth and taste so desirable sites for private residences. The slope of the mountain side is adorned with costly dwellings, which have sprung up as if by magic, and they furnish quiet retreats for the man of business and toil. Men have grown rich in the traffic of our youthful city, and have sought retirement here. This slope commands a delightful view of the busy city below, and the blue waters of the bay and lake beyond. Here is our "Fifth Avenue," and far superior it is to the famous gathering place of the millionaires of New York city. *Their* prospect is limited to massive walls and paved streets, while we look upon a beautiful country and bright waters.[16]

Despite the view and attraction of Hamilton, parts of the west end were still swamp. The swamp included the area a little west of Dundurn Street, around the base of the mountain and the land that connected downtown (where Highway 403 runs today) to the Village of Westdale, as well as other parts of Westdale. By 1857, some of that swamp had been filled and people were quickly settling on the new land.

Hamilton experienced a peak year for tourism in 1857. The train brought settlers, a new connection to other parts of Canada and the United States, as well as a new emergence of wealth and industry.

Unfortunately just a few years before the revival, Hamilton had a serious epidemic of cholera (a form of dysentery caused by bacterial contamination in the drinking water that was often fatal in those days before modern medicine). Some said it came from the immigrants

15. Weaver, *Hamilton: An Illustrated History*, 41–77. See also Shephard, *1858 City of Hamilton Directory*, 4–7, 12, 32.

16. Shephard, *1858 City of Hamilton Directory*, 11.

travelling by train or boat, while others said it came because the waters were polluted. Hamilton's death toll was high from this epidemic. Every morning wagons would go through the city streets collecting the dead to bury them in a mass grave on Burlington Heights. Dead animals were taken to the city dump to rot. Both farmers and merchants feared to go into the city, thus halting almost all commerce. It took a while for Hamilton to recoup its losses and find a solution.

However, in 1857, the Hamilton beach pump house was created with state-of-the-art technology and hydraulics, pumping healthy fresh water into the city once again.[17] In 1860, the Prince of Wales would inaugurate the pump house during his Canadian tour.

Believe it or not, despite the epidemic, Hamilton had just experienced seven years of prosperity and was about to embark on seven years of depression.[18] The battle would continue to rage even stronger for Hamilton's reputation and recognition.

The Bad Times in Hamilton (1857–64)

The year 1857 marked the beginning of seven years of worldwide economic depression. Hamilton had an extremely difficult start to this depression, and the final years would prove no different. During the last years of the depression the city had a difficult time even lighting street lamps in the evening hours. There was a reduction in the police force, and 20 percent loss in both population and business.[19]

Hamilton became stiff competition for Toronto as they were roughly equal in importance. In 1847, Toronto was upset that Hamilton was host to the Provincial Show. The show was similar to an agriculture fair that judged such things as the best farm animals, seeds, crops, and crafted materials. This prestigious show attracted important people such as the Governor General. In an article posted in the Toronto *Globe* newspaper on September 25, 1847, the editor, in a tongue-in-cheek manner, called Hamilton the "ambitious little city."[20] Clearly, despite his feelings, he encouraged people to go and show a good face to the VIPs that would attend, despite the fact that it was not in Toronto. The coined

17. James, "Hamilton's Old Pumphouse."

18. Weaver, *Hamilton: An Illustrated History*, 41–77.

19. Ibid. See also Watson and MacDonald, *History of Hamilton and District*, chs. 20 and 25.

20. "The Ontario Provincial Exhibition," *The Globe*, September 25, 1847, 2.

phrase "ambitious little city" would come to characterize the tension between Hamilton and Toronto for over 150 years.[21] To add insult to injury, many prominent leaders of other cities started looking for ways to by-pass Hamilton with the railroad in order to ensure that the train brought quick wealth to their cities. Fortunately their deals went sour, as the railways were in extreme debt and could not afford the expenditure for such an endeavor.

Desjardins Canal Accident Lithograph

On March 12, 1857 the next tragedy came. A train traveling from Oakville to Hamilton derailed due to a broken spoke because of faulty workmanship. The train carrying ninety passengers was sent plummeting 20 meters (about 60 feet) over the Desjardins Canal Bridge into the frozen waters below, killing fifty-nine people (one of whom was a pastor named Alfred Booker, from Park Street Baptist Church in Hamilton, who was returning home from preaching in Burlington, a neighboring city to Hamilton).[22] For a long time, that incident was to be known as the worst train wreck in Canada, making headlines far and wide. The Hamilton Mayor, John Francis Moore, declared a day of "humiliation and prayer" to remember this tragic event that took the lives of so ma-

21. Henley, *1846 Hamilton*, 142.
22. Ruggle, "Booker, Alfred."

ny.[23] Due to the horrific nature of this accident, passengers feared their journey into Hamilton. It was a long time before people chose not to disembark the train at the Desjardins Canal, cross the bridge on foot, and re-board on the other side.

23. Bailey, *Dictionary of Hamilton Biography*, 156.

3

Methodist Revivals and the Uniqueness of the Hamilton Revival

NEIL SEMPLE'S BOOK *The Lord's Dominion: The History of Canadian Methodism* provides some understanding of how the Methodist Church of those times both lived and interacted with society while maintaining their biblical ideals. Perhaps it was these standards or ideals in part that made the 1857 Hamilton, Ontario Revival so effective. Maybe the people could relate to those sharing the good news because they may not have been viewed as being as peculiar as other Christian denominations that separated themselves from the world in extreme ways. Semple shares how the Methodists conducted themselves:

> What then was a Methodist? In Wesley's own words, "A Methodist is one who has 'the love of God shed abroad in his heart by the Holy Ghost given unto him'; one who 'loves the Lord God with all his heart, and with all his soul, and with all his mind, and with all his strength.' God is the joy of his heart, and the desire of his soul." Methodists did not withdraw behind peculiarities of speech or dress, nor did they differentiate their community by narrowly defined scriptural doctrine. They accepted all the fundamental Protestant beliefs and desired simply to keep God's commandments. They were recognized by their deep spiritual fervour, hard work, sobriety and extent of their charitable acts. Methodism never desired to create an isolated utopian community; they were to avoid contamination by the world's evils yet Christians were to live in the world. Methodism was a vital, expanding fellowship embracing all who "wished to flee from the wrath to come."[1]

1. Semple, *The Lord's Dominion*, 16.

Unlike the Mennonites or Quakers, the Methodists were required to be in the world, but not of it. They were to relate to all people, because all people need a relationship with God. The Methodist's proper boundaries to live in the world required denouncing dancing, popular amusements, and drinking; however they did not separate themselves from others. Instead, they sought different social activities to build community with those who wished to connect with them.[2] This method of living, I believe, aided them to reach out to non-Christians, despite the fact that sometimes it caused tension with other denominations, as well as tension among the Methodist denominations (that may have had different versions of proper living in the world). Occasionally, the Methodist Church required conversations with their members, addressing appropriate apparel and manners.[3] Despite their denunciations, Semple says, "it should be emphasized that Methodism was not a joyless, puritanical retreat from the world."[4] Overall, Methodists sought as their highest mandate the salvation of humankind despite their differences both within Methodism and with other denominations.

During the 1800s there were several branches of Methodism in Canada, but with the same mandate to bring the message of Christ throughout the world, changing entire nations. The branches differed on strategies and methods of accomplishing the mandate. Their differences also lay in their allegiance to Europe, or how strong their ties were to the Anglican Church, how they would conduct relationships with American Methodists (after the war of 1812), and how true they wanted to remain to Wesley's vision.[5] Notwithstanding these internal differences, Methodists grappled with these issues, in order that the Canadian Methodist churches could rise to meet the needs of local people (whites and natives) as well as people of multi-cultural and diverse religious backgrounds. Despite their differences, each of the Methodist denominations still recognized the other Methodist branches as family.[6] Some people would from time to time leave one branch and become a member of another, depending on where their thoughts and allegiances were.[7]

2. Ibid., 56.

3. Ibid., 87.

4. Ibid., 56.

5. Fayter, interview. See also Semple, *The Lord's Dominion*, chs. 1 and 4.

6. Semple, *The Lord's Dominion*, 26.

7. Ibid., 74.

John Wesley (1703–91), the founder of the Methodist Church, lived during the Age of Reason. He encouraged his followers to have a both rational and logical belief, along with heart engagement. A follower's faith must be rational and balanced, not based on fanatical or ecstatic emotion. All thoughts were to be tested through experience (along with the Scriptures). He believed that through their "spiritual senses," all people could know God's will. Semple states, "This concept was critical; the individual not only sensed an external experience, but in fact was transformed by it. It was not sufficient to recognize God's presence; experience created a new person who thus became an agent of God's love."[8] The religious experience of encountering God during revival meetings, as described in Westfall's book *Two Worlds: The Protestant Culture of Nineteenth Century Ontario*, was often the "warming of the heart" by the presence of God, and "breaking the hard shell of sin and giving the soul liberty." For some that disagreed with revival meetings, this encounter with God was often too emotional; however, they could not discount what was occurring in the person or the change of the person after the encounter.[9] The new changes in people would in turn draw the converts into action, sharing their experience, thus fulfilling the mandate of both the Bible and the Methodist Church to spread the gospel to all people.

Richard Carwardine, in his book *Transatlantic Revivalism: Popular Evangelicalism in Britain and America, 1790–1865*, sheds light on the need for revival as the basic foundation for the Methodist Church. Carwardine describes the Methodist movement's heart to fulfill the Great Commission through the use of revivals.

> Revival was essential to the vital and creative existence of the Methodist church. Every service of worship, every private and social means of grace, every sermon, tract, or prayer was directed to this end. The quest for conversion and entire sanctification was unceasing and compelling; it justified all missionary activity and underlay every attempt to reform character and all ethical conduct. "Methodism was wholeheartedly a revival movement: it had been born of a revival; its churches grew through revivals, its ministers preached revival; its success was talked of in terms of revival. Sometimes, when most of those who were converted were the children of Methodist parents, the revival served to con-

---

8. Ibid., 17.
9. Westfall, *Two Worlds*, 58–59, 75–76.

solidate, but just as frequently it sought to break new territory and reach new pockets of population to achieve overall growth."[10]

Fortunately, the Hamilton Revival did not just affect children of church-goers seeking salvation, but the general public, and those who did not have a solid relationship with God were reached as well. Phyllis Airhart, in her book *Serving the Present Age: Revivalism, Progressivism and the Methodist Tradition in Canada*, further connects the importance of revivals to Methodists, and how their identity was tied to conversions.

> Revivalism gave a distinctive piety to Methodism by shaping its understanding of religious experience, guidelines for personal and public behaviour, expression of religious ideas, and associations for cultivating the religious life. This revivalist piety, even more than doctrine or polity, became the identifying mark of Methodism in that century. Revivalism's emphasis on an experience of personal conversion was critically important in helping Methodists define who they were.[11]

Semple further confirms Airhart's observations, stating that, "As well as the strict preaching of conversion and entire sanctification, the early effectiveness of the specialized evangelists was founded on what Carroll termed 'admirable revival tactics.' It seems these men and women knew from training and experience how to draw in their audience, how to build up and sustain the emotional energy, and how to direct the penitent to that critical moment of decision."[12] You can read more about revival tactics in Semple's book, and the scrutiny of the Methodists revivals in Westfall's book. Westfall provides more details of non-Methodist thoughts on the subject. Since Hamilton was part of the "burned over district," the Methodists' balanced views on emotion became part of what I believe to be an important element in the revival in Hamilton, as it was unique with its lack of ecstatic emotion.[13]

In most revivals there are those who hear the words of the good news, but allow only a small amount of change in their lives, often due to their lifestyle or circumstances. Semple goes on to describe what that looked like, as it was practiced during revival meetings:

10. Carwardine, *Transatlantic Revivalism*, 10.

11. Airhart, *Serving the Present Age*, 4.

12. Semple, *The Lord's Dominion*, 142.

13. See the section "Setting the Stage: Worldwide" in chapter 2 above for the definition of the "burned over district."

> After this conversion experience, the "reborn" were usually in-
> terviewed by the revival leaders in order for the conversions to
> be authenticated and enumerated. Critics of revivals had long
> claimed that the conversions were transitory and the numbers
> wildly distorted. However, nearly every report about revivals
> makes it clear that the new converts were carefully examined
> and as much as possible, their change of heart verified. Detailed
> statistics were kept, and attempts were made to measure the in-
> creases in the surrounding congregations.[14]

Westfall addresses what else the Methodists did to minimize the attrition of converts from revivals: "As revivals drew more and more people into the ranks of Methodism, the church had to create new kinds of religious institutions to accommodate the multitudes, and new styles of worship to meet the needs of new groups. The church no longer concentrated exclusively on converting the sinners but now tried also to sustain and cultivate the saved."[15]

The Methodists were keen on the laity developing their spiritual training. Bands were developed by Wesley in 1738 for intimate and spiritually intense groups of Christians who wanted to grow in their faith and learn how to share with others. Then "class" meetings were added for those who were seeking to become Christians.[16] These things were extremely important to keep Christians growing in their faith and give them the stability they needed, and to build the local church that had agreed to participate in the mandate of the Great Commission. William Westfall explains how the Methodists were viewed by some in their evangelism techniques and regarding what was considered their informal education:

> He [John Strachan, the Anglican Rector of York in Upper Canada
> in 1825] compared the settled, well-educated, and sober-minded
> clergy of his own church and the Church of Scotland with the
> emotional, poorly trained Methodist preachers who wandered
> through the colony, disrupting in the name of salvation the slow
> and careful work of redemption that his church was trying so
> hard to carry out. He further suggested that the American ori-
> gins of some of these preachers raised serious doubts about the
> social and political implications of their religious teachings. His

14. Semple, *The Lord's Dominion*, 134.
15. Westfall, *Two Worlds*, 24.
16. Semple, *The Lord's Dominion*, 19.

specific charges form but a small part of his general discourse, and they flow logically from his overall argument: they were sound, reasonable, and perfectly overall consistent. But others saw them very differently, and removed his phrases from their theological context, giving them a prominence they still enjoy. These Methodists were "uneducated itinerant preachers, who leaving their steady employment, betake themselves to preaching the Gospel from idleness, or a zeal without knowledge, by which they are induced without any preparation to teach what they do not know, and which from pride, they disdain to learn."[17]

It was not only the preachers who were targeted by these comments, but also the laity, for the Methodists believed that all were to do their part to fulfill the Great Commission. It would appear that the Methodists paid very little attention to the criticisms, and would continue on their mandate despite the challenges they faced. As Semple said:

It was the laity who withstood ridicule and sometimes mob violence after the preachers had departed. In particular, women supplied a disproportionate leadership in organizing classes and prayer groups, building connexional facilities, and sharing the vision of a new world in Christ. Through word and example, unordained men and women spread Wesley's message of salvation and entire sanctification throughout Britain and carried it as part of their precious luggage whey they emigrated. They became true Christian evangelists, encouraging family and friends to abandon evil and to join the Methodist community.

Many of the more talented men and women became official exhorters who assisted the preachers in expounding the need for an immediate, personal commitment to God and creating a kinship of believers. After gaining practice and being tested as to their "gifts and graces," particularly to show that their exhorting was being blessed with victories, some became lay preachers.[18]

Westfall explains that Egerton Ryerson (a prominent Methodist who lived in Hamilton and had an exciting career in the church, politics, and education) often fought the words aimed against the Methodist lay workers that faulted them for being uneducated.

Instead of describing the training that an itinerant received and the close supervision that the senior members of the Methodist

17. Westfall, *Two Worlds*, 24.

18. Semple, *The Lord's Dominion*, 20–21.

Church exercised over their prospective preachers, he chose instead to argue that education was not necessary. While formal learning might be useful and pleasing, it could never replace the necessity of experiencing the transforming power of the spirit. A preacher must be redeemed; education was a secondary consideration. He turned Strachan's words on their head: knowledge without zeal was a positive evil.[19]

Both Strachan and Ryerson had valid points. Westfall sums it up this way: "As both Strachan and Ryerson show so clearly, religion is not restricted to what goes on in a church [building and meetings]: the way these men (and so many others) saw God also shaped the way they saw the world."[20] So, in any way that they could, the Methodists, whether formally educated or not, continued to share the gospel.

Methodists tried to be inclusive and break down the barriers of denomination in order to achieve the Great Commission. Generally other denominational pastors and congregations were welcomed to attend their events and services.[21] (Bush does note that the Methodist Church did struggle with the doctrines of the Catholic Church, and often wrote about it in their newspapers. He goes on to say that the Methodist relationships with Protestant denominations were more amicable.)[22] Although the invitation to participate in revivals was always open, it was not always accepted. We see this battle even today, as churches struggle with denominational barriers, and not all Christians desire to intermingle with others. An additional reason that different denominations did not always attend Methodist revivals was the fear of "flock stealing," as described by Westfall:

When a revival drew off a large part of an Anglican congregation, the local [Anglican] missionary often railed against the evil excesses of religious enthusiasm, lamenting the lack of firm religious principles among his flock. If the people were only more rational they would not be caught up in such dangerous extravagances. At the same time, Methodist itinerants were continually frustrated by the regrettable tendency of the newly converted to "backslide" or fall away from Methodism after a revival had run its course. Where these backsliders might end up is not certain,

19. Westfall, *Two Worlds*, 26–27.

20. Ibid., 28.

21. Semple, *The Lord's Dominion*, ch. 6. See also Westfall, *Two Worlds*, 58–62.

22. Bush, "James Caughey, Phoebe and Walter Palmer," 78–79.

but from Anglican accounts it is clear that large numbers of them simply went back to their former churches.[23]

Although Westfall addresses the issue of Methodist revivals in regard to backsliders, there is room for further research here. I would agree that to some extent new converts can easily return to their old ways when a revival is finished, especially if there are other factors such as ties to old habits, lack of support, lack of understanding, and lack of continued interest, etc.[24] However, Westfall's words beg the following to be discovered: did those attending the Methodist revivals really leave their church, or perhaps did they not agree with their leadership's thoughts and wanted to check out the revivals for themselves? Were they truly backsliders in their own denomination or just curious on-lookers? Did they go back to be stronger Christians in their own denominations?

My research is inconclusive as to how many congregants from other denominations attended the 1857 Hamilton Revival or how many "backslid" afterwards, but we know the main churches that participated. I suspect that there was very little involvement from other denominations, based upon the documents I have been able to gather. Nevertheless, the Hamilton Revival impacted the city and played a significant role, as Phoebe Palmer was used to help spearhead it and carry the news of the revival to others in her networks throughout the Second Great Awakening.

THE UNIQUENESS OF THE 1857 HAMILTON REVIVAL

Now that the foundation has been laid as to the history of the time, the culture and beliefs of Wesleyan Methodism, and revivals in general, we can move on to the Hamilton Revival specifically. The uniqueness of the 1857 Hamilton Revival can be noted in the fact that it was totally spontaneous; there had been no planning. It was a rare occurrence that started out of a completely natural event for the Methodists of Hamilton. Semple notes how the Methodists usually planned for such events:

> [M]ass evangelistic campaigns were rarely spontaneous occurrences. God's miraculous intervention in the lives of sinners was not needed for revivals to occur. Indeed, revival was believed to be a natural event based on well-organized, cooperative action

23. Westfall, *Two Worlds*, 46–47.
24. Semple, *The Lord's Dominion*, 214.

and "the result of a union effort on the part of spiritually inten-sified individuals." . . . Planning, piety, and determined action brought revival to the community.[25]

Along this line, Peter Bush claims that the Hamilton Revival was wanted and therefore organized; however, there is strong evidence to support that it was not organized according to Methodist standards. In Bush's thesis he details how through desire, prayer, and preaching, revivals would come.[26] He also shows the connections of the three main Hamilton ministers, who each spent time working alongside of revival evangelists such as the Palmers and James Caughey. This would have strengthened the effectiveness and laid the foundation for the Hamilton Revival. The ministers' training and experience would allow them to be able to handle the revival, organize the laity, and continue the work.

> Although the laity was crucially important in this revival, the three Wesleyan Methodist ministers on the Hamilton circuit must have helped push things ahead. Samuel Rice had seen Caughey at work in Kingston and had aided the Palmers in Oakville; obviously he was not opposed to revivals. E. B. Harper had been a Methodist minister in Toronto while Caughey was there and then had gone to Hamilton to help Caughey in 1853. Finally, Charles Lavell had been in Kingston when Caughey had visited in 1852 and 1853; and Lavell was appointed to the same circuit as E. B. Harper. Thus the three ministers in Hamilton had been involved in large revivals led by visiting Americans and they knew how these revivals could be encouraged.[27]

Although people may desire revival, I believe that it is ultimately God who chooses when and to whom to bring it. I believe it helps if one is prepared, but I still believe it is a divine work of God and comes at his timing. Since there were no formal plans laid down to host a re-vival meeting, the Palmers were not intending to stay in Hamilton, and Phoebe's claims that she sensed God's purpose for these unscheduled meetings only as events unfolded reinforces this premise.

What also made the Hamilton Revival unique was that there was no meeting for mass participation of sinners in one place. Westfall de-

25. Ibid., 145.
26. Bush, "James Caughey, Phoebe and Walter Palmer," 56–61.
27. Ibid., 128.

scribes the importance of Methodist revivals and what should be accomplished in planning and during a revival meeting:

> According to contemporary accounts, revivals and camp meetings were distinguished by mass participation: "revivals and camp meetings bring a great number of sinners together." Secondly, revivals were able to isolate these sinners from the world and subject them to a continuous flood of religion: "there is much to be expected from the repeated attacks of divine truth on the minds of sinners at camp meetings, without opportunity of bringing the pleasures of the world in contact with the impressions made thereby." And thirdly, this flood of religion was highly emotional, playing directly upon the feelings and passions of sinners. The result was immediate and powerful conversion: "the animal sympathies of sinners are excited, under the influence of which they are placed in a hearing mood, and in this way often become truly convicted."[28]

Those in attendance at the Hamilton 1857 Revival became the revival preachers, as they left the church, and brought the gospel in their own words to the people they came in contact with on the streets. Although Methodists were actively involved in sharing their faith, at revival meetings it was usually the leadership who did most of the evangelism. The Hamilton Revival was not a normal Methodist revival meeting for the time, for it was not a group of trained religious professionals leading others to a relationship with God at a meeting. I also venture to guess that not every Christian during the Hamilton revival had their theology so well thought out that they could preach the same way the revival preachers could. They just went with a commitment to spread the gospel, an invitation, and what was in their heart. As a result of their actions, this became a revival led by the laity.

Another unique feature for the Hamilton Revival is the fact that although there was a meeting with some preaching, the call to action for the Christians was unemotional or lacking excessive emotion. This was unusual for Methodists during this time. Describing what the usual revival preaching was like, and the charge of the preacher, Westfall says the following:

---

28. Westfall, *Two Worlds*, 40. Westfall takes his information from "The Great Utility of Camp Meetings in Promoting Revivals of Religion," *The Christian Guardian*, 31 October 1832, 201.

> The preaching was intense and emotional; the texts were drawn from some of the most highly charged passages of scripture. In the language of revivals, the preachers had to "preach Christ crucified"; they had to "preach for a verdict," not to inform and instruct but to bring about an immediate conversion to Christ. This conversion experience was itself amazingly intense. As preacher followed preacher, as exhorters moved through the crowds, as the converted turned upon the unrepentant but wavering sinner, individuals would finally break under the weight of revival, acknowledge their sinfulness, and accept God's saving grace.[29]

As noted, revivals or mass evangelism conducted by the Methodist Church often came with emotionalism and scrutiny from outsiders. Westfall explains his view of the value of emotions:

> Although this style of religion was highly emotional, the techniques used by the revivalists had their own rationality. The preacher ascended to exalted height; the people burst into shouts and tears; the preachers responded immediately with prayers and supplication; people were saved. Viewed in this way, revivals were systematic and well conceived. They set out to achieve an emotional encounter with God, and they used the most effective means to this end. That explains in large part why Methodists argued that revivals, in spite of their emotion, were well-ordered and well-managed affairs. There was a certain order within the seeming chaos of emotional religion.[30]

Semple explores the human emotion aspect when discussing both the laity and leadership of the Methodist Church. The following is what I believe to be a key ingredient in revival situations, and as believers grow in their Christian journey. It is an explanation of Wesley's views and use of emotion in revival settings.

> Wesley's understanding of experience must not be confused with irrational "enthusiasm," so anathema to eighteenth-century religious and secular leaders. He was always conscious of the excesses that enthusiasm could generate and was initially shocked at overly emotional responses to his preaching. Emotion was itself legitimate, but he warned that enthusiasts were too often fooled by a false sense of salvation or failed to live holy lives. Some mistakenly felt that God gave them special powers or intervened in

29. Westfall, *Two Worlds*, 40.
30. Ibid., 57–58.

their lives in trivial ways. They therefore believed that they were not obliged to participate in the divinely appointed means of grace. Emotion was a legitimate by-product of experience only when it confirmed and augmented, not irrationally dominated, true rational experience. Wesley came to accept that emotion was as much a part of human nature as reason, and if God chose to use it, he could not deny the beneficial results. Nevertheless, it must be carefully monitored and controlled.[31]

As human beings we need to rely on both our minds and our emotions to guide us. When we are guided by the mind or emotion alone, forgetting to use them in balance, we can sometimes find ourselves in problematic situations. I believe that God created us with both mind and emotion in order to bring balance to our lives. Our emotions help us not to become so cold and rational that we miss the spirit of what is going on around us. Our mind helps our emotions not to sway so far from reality that we base everything on our senses rather than rationality. I believe that by using these two in balance, John Wesley and the Methodists had an excellent understanding of what was needed to reach out to others, especially when it came to revivals and maturing people in their faith. In fact there are some accounts of believers who discredited emotion, but when attending revival meetings themselves, they saw the value, as they used both their head and their heart to discern what they understood as God's moving.

Although perhaps not totally unique in nature, but still unusual when compared with other revivals that had happened that summer, the Hamilton Revival was upheld as a model for other Christians to copy. In Phoebe Palmer's letter written to her "Beloved Sister T," published in the Methodist newspaper *The Christian Guardian* of Wednesday December 2, 1857, she says:

> This revival is, by the blessing of God, the result of a *"Laity for the Times."* A *Ministry for the Times* is all-important, but it does not take the place of a *Laity for the Times.* Our good Ministers here speak of it as a MODEL REVIVAL and never have we witnessed a revival that might so worthily be enstamped with this appellation.[32]

31. Semple, *The Lord's Dominion*, 17–18.
32. Palmer, "A Revival after Apostolic Times."

In the same letter, Phoebe continues with her hopes of this Hamilton Revival becoming something that could become a pattern used to convert sinners all over the world. Little did she know at the time of writing that the revival would spread and turn into the Great Awakening, as Christians began to seek God's will.

> It is also a revival after the fashion of *primitive Wesleyan Times*. "They are all at it and always at it." So said an eminent Divine, as characteristic of the early Methodists. Methodism might indeed be distinguished as "Christianity in earnest," if such a revival might become general in Europe and America. Everywhere, where Methodists of this sort might plant themselves might it be said, "These men which turn the world upside down, have come hither also."
>
> And in other respects, beyond what I have room to state, is this model revival. The church is apprehending the importance of conformity to *Scripture!* And *Wesleyan* views in regard to the use of every diversity of talent. The necessity of bringing all the tithes into the Lord's store-house is being recognized.[33]

It is also interesting to note that surviving documentation on the Hamilton Revival seems to attribute the initiating of the revival to Phoebe Palmer's leadership. The role of women in the 1800s was beginning to change. At the start of Methodism, the roles for women were very defined, as well as the way they were to be carried out. Women were not overly encouraged to be in the forefront of public ministry roles. Evangelism, however, since it was central to Methodism, was a key activity for women. Airhart describes this in the following way:

> Conversion was central to the piety of both men and women in Canadian Methodist circles. For women it was tied to a concept of "evangelical womanhood" which shaped the way that women aspiring to it formed friendships and chose activities.
>
> Conversion became for them the defining experience of their lives; it marked the beginning of a commitment to nurturing the Christian life that involved intensive self-examination of daily activities and "useful" social involvement.[34]

Slowly the roles that women could participate in both in the church and in revival meetings began to increase. Methodist women began to

33. Ibid.

34. Airhart, *Serving the Present Age*, 21.

exercise roles as laity (unordained leadership) at the congregational level: in worship, exhortation, and in their ability to complement or expand the work of regular itinerants (as long as they kept a low profile). They led women's missionary societies and mass evangelism efforts, and could speak publicly on issues such as abolition and other issues that affected the family unit such as the temperance movement. (Lack of temperance affected women and their children, and opposition to alcohol consumption was considered a form of home protection.)[35]

During the Hamilton Revival, according to Phoebe Palmer, she heard the will of God, spoke it to encourage the Christians, and led them forth to take hold of revival. In accordance with the roles of women in the Methodist Church at the time, Phoebe was using her influence and operating in the appropriate traditional role for women during a prayer meeting. The fact is, she did spearhead a large revival, as many testify. It was her words that seem to have taken more root in the hearts of men and women than any prayer or preaching did the first night, and during the nights that followed. It would almost appear that her words became more influential than the words of a sermon, as she believed they were directly from God. Although she still acted within the bounds of Methodist policies, it was an exciting phenomenon that Phoebe could be credited with. Phoebe was inspired by her role model, the late John Wesley. He was the founder of Methodism, who sought to include women in ordination for four main reasons: the advice of his mother Susanna (who was the main influence in his own conversion), seeking to be in alignment with Scripture, the arguments of gifted women, and lastly, his own experience with the value and calling of women in ministry.[36] During her life, Phoebe Palmer was very influential in advocating change for the role of women in leadership within the church (including ordination and preaching), most likely because of her successes and influence.

Lastly, Phoebe had taken hold of the Wesleyan doctrine of "entire sanctification" that was popularized during this Great Awakening. The practice of entire sanctification encouraged Christians to utilize the power of the Holy Spirit and his gifts immediately after conversion, or

35. Whiteley, *Canadian Methodist Women*, ch. 4. See also Semple, *The Lord's Dominion*, 120, 144.

36. Semple, *The Lord's Dominion*, 21. See also Wheatley, *Life and Letters of Mrs. Phoebe Palmer*, and Dayton and Dayton, "Your Daughters Shall Prophesy," 68–70.

as soon as possible, in order that they could immediately sense what God's will for them was, so they could continue to keep perfecting their Christian journey. Semple emphasizes Mrs. Palmer's view in the following passage:

> Methodism believed in the necessity of a personal experience of conversion and a rebirth to a life in Jesus Christ as Lord and Saviour. This rebirth was to be followed by the constant quest for a sanctified life totally committed to the love of God and humankind. Methodism in all its personal and social dimensions remained profoundly dedicated to the whole range of elements that composed spiritual and moral Christianity. Everything belonged to God; there should be no division between the sacred and the secular world. Thus Methodism endeavored to assist everyone ultimately to achieve heaven and to transform all of society into heaven on earth.[37]

Phyllis Airhart gives a good synopsis of how Phoebe Palmer handled entire sanctification:

> By placing "all upon the altar," she had been able to claim the scriptural promise of Matthew 23:19—that the altar sanctified the gift, cleansing the believer of sin that remained after conversion. This was "a shorter way" to holiness, she argued, than that proposed by those who viewed the pursuit of perfection as a lifelong process.[38]

In the end, despite the popularity of entire sanctification teaching, the blessing of the Holy Spirit did not prevent backsliding.[39] Despite the factions in the Methodist Church over this doctrine, it did become popular with many Methodists as well as with other Protestant denominations. Smith writes about what the other denominations thought of the issue:

> When revival broke out, it seemed to its champions a "modern Pentecost" in which the "gift of power" bestowed upon believers of every sect was preparing the way for the conversion of the world and the early advent of the kingdom of God on earth. "We need the gift of the Spirit, and we need it now," wrote James W. Alexander at its height; "we need it to break the power of sin in

37. Semple, *The Lord's Dominion*, 8.
38. Airhart, *Serving the Present Age*, 22.
39. Semple, *The Lord's Dominion*, 139, 141, 220–21.

professing Christians and to nail their lusts to the cross." The phe-
nomenal success of William E. Boardman's volume, *The Higher
Christian Life*, published at the height of the awakening, can only
be explained in terms of the universal awareness of this want.
No wonder that Dr. and Mrs. Palmer found Baptist, Presbyterian,
and Congregational pulpits thrown open to them that summer!
Apostolic unction was the burden of every prayer. At an all-day
union meeting in Baltimore in 1859 prominent pastors of nearly
every denomination joined in urging a distinct experience of
baptism of the Holy Spirit subsequent to conversion.[40]

For more information on the subject of entire sanctification I suggest
reading Timothy Smith's book *Revivalism and Social Reform: American
Protestantism on the Eve of the Civil War*, or Phyllis Airhart's book
*Serving the Present Age: Revivalisim, Progressivism and the Methodist
Tradition in Canada* (chapter 1), as well as Marguerite Van Die's *An
Evangelical Mind: Nathanael Burwash and the Methodist Tradition in
Canada, 1839–1918* (chapter 3 on Christian Perfection).

---

40. Smith, *Revivalism and Social Reform*, 135–36.

4

Hamilton Churches and Pastors in 1857

HAMILTON CHURCHES

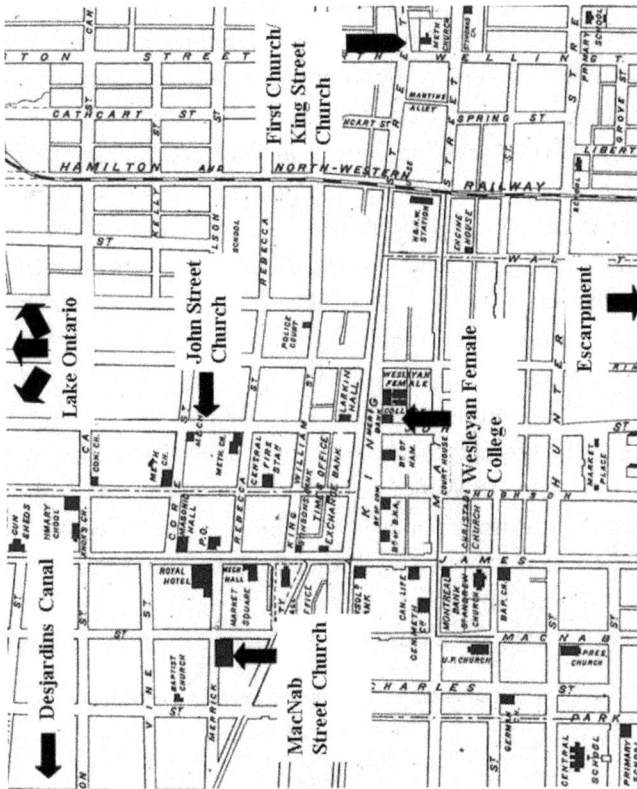

Map of Hamilton showing location of the three churches
participating in the revival

There were several large and small mainline churches in Hamilton in 1857: Baptist, Anglican, Presbyterian, Methodist, Congregational, and Roman Catholic. Among the listings there were two African-Canadian churches, known then as "coloured" churches: one Baptist, one Methodist Episcopal.[1] As a point of interest, the Masonic Lodge had an establishment on the corner of James Street North and Gore Street (known today as Wilson Street), a little over a block away from the birthplace of the revival. Although many of the churches have changed or disappeared, you can still see some of the structures built around 1857 today (please refer to the section titled *Hamilton* in chapter 1). A high percentage of the Hamilton churches bore the name Methodist. Methodist denominations in Hamilton included the Wesleyan, Episcopal, and Primitive Methodists, as well as other off-shoots. There were at least five and perhaps as many as eleven or more Methodist churches of various kinds within the city limits.[2] (It is difficult to get a true count, as some churches were home-based, and not all maps marked all churches.) These Methodist churches were led by some prominent ministers of their time, such as William Case, Egerton Ryerson, and Samuel Rice.[3]

There were two Christian periodicals produced in Hamilton in 1857, as noted by the *Hamilton Directory*.[4] One was the *Canada Evangelist*, a monthly evangelical paper published by Rev. Robert Peden (formerly Presbyterian) of the Evangelical Union Church.[5] The other was the *Canada Christian Advocate*, which was "A weekly Religious and Family Journal for the Methodist Episcopal Church."[6] The *Canada Christian Advocate* appears to have recorded only revival events as they occurred in the United States, and not in Hamilton. This may be due to the fact that the paper was published by the Episcopal Methodists, and the churches hosting the Hamilton Revival were Wesleyan Methodists. It seems very unfortunate that a revival of this importance in Hamilton did not affect them. In fact, on October 17, 1857 (about a week after the Hamilton Revival had begun) an article appeared on the second page, titled "Why There Is No More Revival." The article gave a number of reasons for the lack of revival, in-

---

1. Shephard, *1858 City of Hamilton Directory*, 10–11, 22–23.

2. Ibid. This number includes other Methodist denominations besides the Wesleyans.

3. Davis, *Centennial Souvenir of First Methodist Church*, 13, 36–37.

4. Shephard, *1858 City of Hamilton Directory*, 32.

5. McGregor-Clewes, "Peden, Rev. Robert."

6. Shephard, *1858 City of Hamilton Directory*, 32.

cluding lack of persevering prayer, lack of faith, the efforts of the church that had not been directed to accomplish revival, and the need for both preaching and preachers to be holy as an example to others.[7]

It is sad that similar problems can exist in the church today. People can be closed to understanding the work of God in sister churches and other denominations; people (and publications) make judgment calls (right or wrong) on what they feel is important to local history, and it is still possible that those keeping records do not recognize the significance of events occurring in their own time. However, I believe that whether we choose to ignore, discount, or keep records of what God is doing, God will still move and do what he wants and needs to do. The Christian publications that carried the news of the revival were published by the Wesleyan Methodists.

In her book *The Promise of the Father*, Phoebe Palmer referred to the participating churches when speaking about the revival: "*The membership in Hamilton, comprising the three Wesleyan churches, has heretofore numbered about five hundred.*"[8] The churches involved with the revival had origins as a part of the Wesleyan Methodist Preaching Circuit. The Hamilton Wesleyan Methodist Circuit included four locations: the King Street church (also known as the First Methodist Church), John Street church (also known as the Wesleyan Church), the MacNab Street church (also known as the MacNab Street Methodist Church), and the Main Street church, which was probably at that time a location run by the John Street church.

In the Hamilton Wesleyan Methodist Circuit records, I could not find the exact location of the Main Street church. However, listed in the *1858 City of Hamilton Directory* for the Wesleyan Methodists are three pastors and five churches.[9] For all five of these churches, only the names of the trustees connected with the churches are given. It is my guess that apart from the three established churches (King Street, John Street, and MacNab Street) the other two may have been missions or Sunday schools, started with the hope that they would grow to become full churches. It is interesting to note that the fifth listing in the *Directory* is for the Main St. West church, which is also listed in the Hamilton Wesleyan Methodist Circuit Records. In addition, an article from the *Hamilton Daily News*

7. "Why There Is No More Revival."

8. Palmer, *Promise of the Father*, 254.

9. Shepard, *1858 City of Hamilton Directory*, 22–23.

of October 15, 1955 states: "The Wesley church started several missions, which became successful churches. The first begun in 1855, on a street in the west end; this became Zion United."[10] This 1855 building, located on Main West and Margaret, was known foremost as a Sunday School and also as a Mission, and was most likely built as a joint effort with the King Street church. A scrapbook on Zion United Church shows an article that states that the Sunday School eventually came under the covering of Centennial Methodist (United) Church, and mentions the fact that there was an appeal to Rev. Samuel Rice to help staff the school.[11] In 1867, the foundation for a new Sunday School and Mission was laid on Napier Street, and services began in the new building in 1868.[12] In 1874 the Sunday School and Mission became a church in its own right, and a church structure was added on Pearl Street.[13] This could be the Main Street church that was a part of the Hamilton Wesleyan Circuit. It may have been mainly used as a Sunday School during the revival period, although the primary sources are vague in the documentation of it.

Zion Methodist Church

10. Baldwin, "City's Wesley United Church Counts History back to '78," 10.

11. "Zion Tabernacle Sunday School, Zion United Church Scrapbook," 7.

12. "Zion Sunday School Will Mark 100 Years This Month." *Hamilton Daily News*, November 16, 1955, 17.

13. The date can be verified from a plaque on the outside of the building.

Zion Sunday School

It is very clear that the John Street church and the MacNab Street church were involved in the revival, and they were Wesleyan Methodist congregations. Since one of the pastors involved with the revival is listed as the First Methodist Church pastor, I have concluded that the King Street church was involved, as the third participating church.

The King Street Church

First Methodist Church

The Hamilton Methodists who had been holding worship services in their homes since the late 1790s needed a permanent place of worship. In 1810, Richard Springer, a Methodist, gave his land on the corner of King and Wellington to the Methodist congregation upon which to build a simple log church.[14]

In 1824, the congregation built a larger wooden church on that property. The church became known as the "King Street Wesleyan Church," or the "King Street Church" for short, but it was also known as the "White Church," as the wooden structure was painted white. By 1875, the church became known as "First Methodist Church," indicating that it was the original Methodist church in the city of Hamilton.[15]

The *Dictionary of Hamilton Biography* states that Samuel D. Rice came to Hamilton in 1857, and was the pastor for what would become known as the First Methodist Church until 1864.[16] Most likely the First Methodist Church was the headquarters for the Hamilton Wesleyan Methodist Circuit Preachers, but since the *Dictionary of Hamilton Biography* states that Rice was the pastor, we can be assured that this church was part of the revival. Furthering this speculation is evidence from a letter about the revival that Samuel D. Rice wrote. He indicated that he took a short ramble to the MacNab Street church that hosted the Palmers (whom God used to initiate the revival). Assuming that he started from a church, the shortest ramble would be from either the King Street church or the John Street church (Rev. Rice was overseeing both at the time) and not the Main Street church. Since the King Street church was the first Methodist church in Hamilton, the closest to Rice's home (on Main Street between Walnut and Cherry Street),[17] and the closest church (if it was a toss-up between the Main Street West church and the King Street church) to the location of the revival, it would make sense that the King Street church was one of the three churches involved with the revival.

14. Pawson, *Growing Together*, 7.

15. Ibid., 7–8.

16. Bailey, *Dictionary of Hamilton Biography*, 170.

17. Shephard, *1858 City of Hamilton Directory*, 22, 236.

The John Street Church

John Street Methodist Church Outside

John Street Methodist Church Inside

In 1841, the King Street Wesleyan congregation planted a new church on the corner of Rebecca and John Streets. It was known as the "Wesley

Church" or "Brick Church."[18] The "Brick Church" was ideally situated to be an excellent location for the birthplace for the Hamilton Revival. The *1858 City of Hamilton Directory*, describing John Street, says that it "extending from the bay to the mountain, is sufficiently broad and central to become one of our first streets . . . The stranger visiting Hamilton will not fail to ascend the mountain by this road; for from any point of it, he can obtain a better view of the city and bay, and surrounding country, than from any other position. Besides on this ascending street are located some of our finest residences, and most beautiful grounds."[19]

This large "Brick Church" had a basement, and would become the site where Phoebe and Walter Palmer would see the revival ignite and flourish in Hamilton. Due to the central location of the church, it was used as a primary place for worship when all the churches on the circuit met together. Since it was the only Methodist church at the time with a large basement that housed lecture rooms, we can safely assume it was the church that the revival started in. Acknowledging the Methodist revivals in the past, and perhaps even with a nod to their historic part in 1857, a Centennial Booklet published by Wesley United Church noted, "Many revivals were held during the days of Methodism, which were attended by crowds and with great religious fervor, and were a great help in drawing new members into the congregation. Wesley was also fortunate in its choice of ministers, many of them being foremost of their day."[20]

18. Pawson, *Growing Together*, 8.

19. Shephard, *1858 City of Hamilton Directory*, 10–11, 22–23. "Mountain" refers to the section of the Niagara Escarpment in Hamilton.

20. *Centennial of Wesley United Church, Hamilton ON 1839 to 1939*, 8.

MacNab Street Church

MacNab Street Methodist Church

The MacNab Street church became the third Methodist church and was located on the corner of Merrick and MacNab. It was also known as the "Stone Church." Prior to the revival, the good-sized congregation of MacNab Street church had additional space with extra balconies and galleries, but the renovations had been left incomplete for many years. Since the King Street church was old, in need of repair and a larger building, the MacNab Street church was looked to for interim accommodation for the King Street congregation while the repairs were done. A decision was made to finish construction on the MacNab Street church first to make it big enough for this. Upon its completion in 1851 many King Street congregants moved into the MacNab Street church for two years while the King Street church was repaired. Upon the King Street church's completion, most of the congregation returned back to their former place of worship.[21]

The MacNab Street church made a mark in Hamilton history, not only by participating in the start of the revival, but also by hosting a memorial service for the survivors and families involved in the Desjardins Canal train wreck. The congregation's outreach and love for the community was noted in the local newspaper. True to the giving spirit of this church, the minister(s) of the MacNab Street church invited the Palmers to stay with them for the night when the Palmers' travel plans were delayed. It was an ideal location for the travelers to spend the night,

21. Pawson, *Growing Together*, 9. See also Shephard, *1858 City of Hamilton Directory*, 10–11, 22–23.

as the Hamilton Directory of that time describes MacNab Street as being close to the Farmers Market, James Street, and the Great Western Railway Depot.

HAMILTON MINISTERS

The local Wesleyan Methodist churches shared a tight bond, and were part of the same Methodist Circuit for preaching.[22] The Wesleyan ministers of the city at that time were: Samuel D. Rice (who is listed in several sources as the minister for both the John Street and the King Street churches and also as part of the Hamilton Methodist Leadership), Rev. Ephraim Boyd Harper, and Charles Lavell.[23] The listings for the other Methodist pastors and other denominational pastors of Hamilton can be found in the *1858 City of Hamilton Directory.*

Although Phoebe's letters state that three to four ministers were involved, she does not name them all. Samuel Rice, who was part of the leadership in the Hamilton Methodist Conference of 1857, gave account of the Hamilton revival to the Methodist newspaper, *The Christian Guardian.* Not only was Rice a part of the circuit for the John Street Wesleyan Methodist church, he was a very influential man in the Hamilton area. Other than Rice, we do know that Rev. Ephraim B. Harper followed up with a letter a few months later to let Phoebe know how the work in Hamilton progressed. He is listed in the *1858 City of Hamilton Directory* as a Wesleyan Minister with his home address on Park Street between York and Market Streets.[24] Harper was well-respected for his knowledge and ministry. According to John Carroll's book, *The Conference of Crayons,* he had a large and rare library, and later would become the Chairman of the Canadian Conference. If we go by the publication date of this book, it would appear that he was about 37 years old in 1857. Here is how Carroll describes Harper:

> Mr. H. is just such a preacher as you might expect . . . not oratorical and showy—not loud and boisterous; but evangelical, spiritual, expository, rich in matter, and always opportune and appropriate. A workman he is "who needeth not to be ashamed,

---

22. Hamilton Wesleyan Methodist Circuit Records.

23. Shephard, *1858 City of Hamilton Directory,* 22.

24. Ibid., 22, 204.

rightly dividing the word of the truth" . . . An Irish-Canadian is
he.[25]

Apart from this, there are very few sources that include the names of
the Hamilton ministers that Phoebe worked with and referred to in her
writings.

Samuel Rice (September 1815–December 1884)

Rev. Samuel Rice

Samuel Rice was born in Maine in 1815. His father was a Puritan physician. His family moved to New Brunswick when he was four years old.
He was schooled in Massachusetts, alongside his classmate poet Henry
Wadsworth Longfellow. After several years of a career in commercial
pursuits, he returned to New Brunswick and, having realized the vanity
of his life, was converted at the age of seventeen under the ministry of
Rev. Arthur McNutt.

25. Carroll, "Rev. E. B. Harper," 268.

After his conversion Samuel preached on the Methodist Miramichi Circuit, had a church in St. John, New Brunswick, and worked a year at the Sackville Wesleyan College.

In 1843 he married Miss Starr of Halifax, with whom he had five children. In 1847 he came to Upper Canada, where he settled. He preached at a church on Richmond Street in Toronto, and was appointed to oversee the Muncey Industrial School at Mount Elgin for a year (a Wesleyan Methodist First Nations Residential School, backed by funds raised by Rev. Peter Jones of the First Nations).[26] Eventually he was stationed in Kingston as the Chairman of the District. He became very important to Victoria College, as he became the treasurer and Moral Governor for four years, during their difficult times.

In 1857 he found himself stationed in Hamilton, Ontario. From 1857 to 1864, he was the minister of the King Street church.[27] Samuel was 42 years old when the revival of 1857 started in Hamilton. After two years of active duty he suffered from a throat infection, so he retired for two years, but took a church again in 1862. In 1863 he was appointed Governor of the Wesleyan Female College in Hamilton, Ontario, where he stayed for fifteen years. It was said of him, "During his whole ministerial life, he took a deep interest in the educational work of the Church, and gave much time and effort to awaken people to a deeper sense of its importance."[28]

In the years to follow his Hamilton stint, he would travel to St. Mary's, Winnipeg, Belleville, and back again to Toronto. He would become the President of the General Conference of the Methodist Church of Canada.

Reverend E. H. Dewart, editor for *The Christian Guardian*, on December 17, 1884 wrote about Reverend Rice's effect on Canada. These words honored his passing.

> This rapid glance at the positions which Dr. Rice occupied will show that his was an active and laborious life, and that he

26. "Mount Elgin Industrial Institute."

27. Bailey, *Dictionary of Hamilton Biography*, 170.

28. Dewart, "Samuel Dwight Rice." Note: Semple, *The Lord's Dominion*, 133, says, "Rev. Samuel Rose opened the Dundas Ladies Academy in 1857, but it soon moved to Hamilton, where it merged into the Hamilton Wesleyan Female College. Chartered in 1859, the new school opened two years later and remained an impressive landmark until 1897."

possessed in a high degree the confidence of his brethren who placed him in so many difficult and responsible positions. No man in our Church has for the last thirty years been more prominently connected with the Methodist movements and enterprises of our Canadian Methodism.[29]

"There was no acid or gall in his nature," said an obituary in the 1885 *Canadian Methodist Magazine.*[30] Dewart went on in the *Guardian* article to describe the attributes of Samuel Rice:

> Dr. Rice was a man of tall and commanding figure, with a strong and intellectual face, a splendid specimen of physical manhood, which makes it easy to believe the feats of courage and endurance reported of his youthful days. His mind corresponded in its active energy and decisive firmness with the physical frame which enshrined it. But, although possessing a self assertion and confidence in his own judgment, that sometimes wore the appearance of sternness, he had a kind heart. We never met a young lady that had been educated under his care at Hamilton, who did not cherish for him a warm regard and affection. He was a man of strong faith and lofty courage. He was always ready to attempt great things for God and his cause. He was ardently attached to the doctrines and usages of Methodism. [His] past achievements made him feel that no enterprise was too great to be undertaken with confident hopes of success [*sic*]. He had large views as to the future of our missionary, educational and literary work, and took a special interest in the business part of Church enterprises. As a presiding officer he was dignified and firm, in later years showing a greater disposition to feel his way cautiously to right conclusions of difficult questions. He was devout and reverent in spirit, an earnest and forcible preacher; and as a pastor and administrator, he evinced his faith in the wisdom of Wesley's counsel, "not to mend our rules, but keep them." . . . He was patriotic and public-spirited; yet he took little part in affairs outside his own Church. He was satisfied to say, like the Shunammite, "I dwell among mine own people."[31]

These accounts show how much Dr. Rice was admired and respected in his time.

29. Ibid.
30. "Current Topics and Events: Death of Rev. Rice."
31. Dewart, "Samuel Dwight Rice."

5

The Palmers

WALTER CLARKE PALMER (1804–83)

Dr. Walter Palmer

Walter Clarke Palmer was born on February 9, 1804, to Miles and Deborah Clarke Palmer in Middletown, New Jersey. In May of that same year his family moved to New York City where he was raised.

He became a Christian at the age of thirteen, and immediately became a Sunday School teacher.[1] After his conversion he struggled with determining whether his calling was to become a minister or a doctor. He finally decided, that "no calling on earth could be more Christlike, in its aims and purposes than that of a pious physician. . . . to possess a correct knowledge of the healing art, so as to know how to go about doing good, not only to the souls of the redeemed race, but to their bodies also."[2] So in July 1826, Walter graduated from Rutgers Medical College of Physicians with honors.

Walter proceeded to open a medical practice and was known for his kindness to those in need. Often he did not charge for his service or medicine—instead he gave out of his own pocket. He was known to give generously, not only to those he met, but to charity and the church. Combining his medical practice with his spiritual desires and tender personality, throughout his career he was able to lead many to Christ as he tended to their physical bodies and spiritual hearts.[3]

Though successful at his career, he did struggle from time to time with the fact that he was unable to help everybody. Likely it was in those times that God reminded him of who the "Great Physician" was, and that he was to point all people to him.

Looking at his life and his work, it seems that God used him in many ways to influence not only the sick and poor, but those who held positions of authority. In Phoebe Palmer's writings, she tells how her husband was invited to read Psalm 91 at President Lincoln's funeral, while a nation grieved over a president's assassination.[4] Phoebe often wrote about other prominent people, including diplomats, that she and her husband entertained.

Walter's love for people was the strongest when it came to one woman: Phoebe Worrall. Many say that it was one of his greatest accomplishments to capture her heart and win the approval of her family, despite her many suitors. The year after Walter's graduation from medical school, on September 28, 1827, he married Phoebe.

1. White, *Beauty of Holiness*, 4.
2. Raser, *Phoebe Palmer*, 32. See also White, *Beauty of Holiness*, 4.
3. Raser, *Phoebe Palmer*, 32.
4. Wheatley, *Life and Letters of Mrs. Phoebe Palmer*, 60–61.

THE WORRALL FAMILY

Henry Worrall was born in England and raised to participate in the national Church of England, as part of the culture of that day. In his teen years, during the night he would sneak out of the house to attend Methodist Society Meetings, with which he believed his parents would disagree. In a meeting in which John Wesley was preaching, he quietly became a Christian, and continued visiting the meetings secretly.[5]

Henry eventually became an engineer and businessman. He sold machinery to factories, which allowed his family to have a comfortable life during the industrial age. He and his family often entertained prominent British diplomats.

Henry married Dorothea Wade, who was also a Methodist, and moved to America. Together they had sixteen children. He taught his children to serve God in everything they did. Phoebe was the fourth of their children to be born.[6]

PHOEBE WORRALL PALMER (1807–74)

Mrs. Phoebe Palmer

5. White, *Beauty of Holiness*, 1–2. See also Raser, *Phoebe Palmer*, 13–14.
6. White, *Beauty of Holiness*, 1–2.

Phoebe (her name means shining and manifest) was known for her devotion to Christ and the purity of her heart. She was an excellent Christian example and had a great fear of lying and disobeying her parents, for which she was sometimes teased. In one of her diaries she wrote, "I do not remember ever to have been willfully disobedient to any parental commands."[7]

Phoebe's writing skills developed early and became helpful in identifying the birthplace of the "Layman's Revival" as Hamilton, Ontario. Phoebe adhered closely to John Wesley's Methodist doctrines and often wrote about issues from the Methodist standpoint. The letters and other writings (books and Methodist newspaper articles) that she composed during her adult years have become a valuable resource to many.

Many of Phoebe's writings indicate the prominent people who were her close friends, many of whom were diplomats or the heads of Christian universities. In *The Beauty of Holiness*, by Charles White, we learn that the British Consul, George Buchanan, presented her with a Bible.[8] In the book *Phoebe Palmer: Selected Writings*, Nathan Bangs is listed as her close friend and the one who taught her the catechism (a series of questions and answers on the principles of Christianity, learned prior to membership, baptism, confirmation, or profession of faith) in 1817.[9] Nathan Bangs was an American Methodist leader who was President of the Wesleyan University from 1841 to 1842, started the Methodist Missionary Society, was an editor for the first Methodist newspaper, the *Christian Advocate*, spent time as a minister both in Canada and New York, and was vocal about the Canadians having their own independent church.[10] Phoebe's love for ministry, Canada, and writing may have provided grounds for a great friendship.

There is a parallel between Phoebe Palmer and the Phoebe of the Bible (Romans 16:1). They were both deaconesses, or, as many would argue, they were more than that: they were both ministers. Both Phoebes were "a succourer of many," which means they were patronesses of the unprotected and despised, ones who came to the aid of converts in need, ones who fought the battles of those who were oppressed.[11] Charles

7. Raser, *Mrs. Phoebe Palmer*, 26. See also White, *Beauty of Holiness*, 2.

8. White, *Beauty of Holiness*, 3.

9. Oden, *Phoebe Palmer: Selected Writings*, 4, 15.

10. Semple, *The Lord's Dominion*, 75.

11. Deen, *All the Women of the Bible*, 230–32.

White's book *The Beauty of Holiness* describes how Phoebe Palmer evangelized: she encouraged people to come to church by offering clothes, food, and money.

Based on her writings and other documents the evidence indicates that Phoebe Palmer took great care to try to walk closely with God in all that she did. When her husband came on the scene she knew that Walter was God's divine choice for her to marry, as he loved God and gained the approval of Phoebe's friends and family. At the end of her life she credited her husband with loving her and helping her to be all that she could be for Christ.

Mrs. Phoebe Palmer

During her last illness, Phoebe declared her undying love for Walter (a love rooted in their mutual love for Christ) and made known the support he was to her. "You have been one of the kindest husbands to me; I could not have done what I have, without you. Our love has been abiding, and it will abide forever. It will be one with Jesus."[12]

12. Wheatley, *Life and Letters of Mrs. Phoebe Palmer*, 24–25.

WALTER AND PHOEBE PALMER—THEIR PERSONAL LIFE AND MINISTRY

At nineteen years of age Phoebe married Walter on September 28, 1827 and settled in Manhattan, New York.[13] As good as their life was, they kept things simple. They were examples of the Methodist faith, not carried away by riches or status. Their home was modest, and a good portion of their time was spent ministering to others. In the book *Life and Letters of Mrs. Phoebe Palmer* their home is described both in looks and feeling:

> It is an ideal METHODIST home—for use and comfort—not at all for show. It is in a section of the city that unites many of the pleasures of the country with all the advantages of the city. That commodious and beloved domicile is dedicated to God . . . "Holiness to the Lord" is written on the walls, and is the moral air in which the inmates live, move, and have their being.[14]

Again, this essence was reflected throughout their life. In a letter dated February 25, 1859 Phoebe describes their sacrifice and motivation for their ministry. "Thus far, our financial affairs have not, in an *earthly* sense, prospered, during our many and long continued absences from home. We have had the *privilege* of testing whether we were willing to sacrifice that which cost us something . . . one soul outweighs millions of silver and gold [coins]."[15]

Upon their first anniversary, Phoebe gave birth to a boy they named Alexander. He died eleven months later.[16] Amidst her grieving, Phoebe believed that God had taken him, her treasure, away so that she could be fully dedicated to God and not have her passions swayed by anything else.[17]

Filled with renewed hope, the next spring she gave birth to Samuel. She believed that God had given him as a replacement for Alexander, so she lived for God fully. Unfortunately he lived only seven weeks. This was extremely difficult for Phoebe, as I am sure it was for Walter.[18]

13. Ibid., 23, 21.
14. Ibid., 150.
15. Ibid., 111.
16. White, *Beauty of Holiness*, 5.
17. Raser, *Phoebe Palmer*, 39.
18. White, *Beauty of Holiness*, 5–6.

Again, she believed that the child was taken away as a result of her own spiritual state that was lacking.[19]

Finally, to the couple's joy, in 1833 a healthy daughter Sarah was born. She lived a full life.[20] Hoping that the worst was behind, Phoebe gave birth to another child named Eliza in August of 1835. The birthing process almost killed Phoebe and Eliza, but fortunately they both survived.[21]

One day a nursemaid was tending to Eliza, who was not more than a year old. She placed the child in her gauze covered bassinette. Noticing that the light needed more oil; she refueled it while it was lit. The oil round the lamp caught fire in her hand. Without thinking she threw the burning lamp away from herself. It landed in the bassinette, quickly igniting it. Phoebe heard the screams of pain from her child and the nursemaid, and quickly ran into the nursery. She doused the flames on Eliza but it was too late. The child was already covered in burns, and only lived a few hours more. Phoebe was devastated. She wrote:

> After the angel spirit winged its way to Paradise, I retired alone, not willing that anyone should behold my sorrow. While pacing the room, crying to God, amid the tumult of grief, my mind was arrested by a gentle whisper, saying, "Your heavenly father loves you. He would not permit such a great trial, without intending that some great good, proportionate in magnitude and weight should result. He means to teach you some great lesson that might not otherwise be learned. He doth not willingly grieve or afflict the children of men. If not *willingly*, then he has some specific design, in this, the greatest of all the trials you have been called to endure."
>
> In the agony of my soul I had exclaimed, "O, what shall I do!" And the answer now came—"Be still, and know that I am God." I took up the precious word, and cried, "O, teach me the lessons of this trial," and the first lines to catch my eye on opening the Bible, were these, "O, the depth of the riches, both of the wisdom and knowledge of God! How unsearchable are his judgments and his ways past finding out!"
>
> It is the Holy Spirit alone that can take the things of God and reveal them to the waiting soul. The tumult of feeling was hushed, and with the words came a divine conviction, that it was a loving

19. Raser, *Phoebe Palmer*, 39–40.

20. White, *Beauty of Holiness*, 7.

21. Ibid., 7, 9.

Father's hand, that had inflicted the stroke. "What thou knowest not now, thou shalt know hearafter," was assuringly whispered. Wholly subdued before the Lord, my chastened spirit nestled in quietness under the wing of the Holy Comforter.

From that moment the very distressing keenness of the trial passed away, and my loved little one, who during her brief stay on earth, had seemed so akin to heaven's inhabitants, appeared scarcely separated from me . . . God takes our treasures to heaven, that our hearts may be there also. My darling is in heaven doing angel service. And now I have resolved, that the service, or in other words, the time I would have devoted to her, shall be spent in work for Jesus.[22]

Phoebe called out to God amidst her pain and suffering for an answer. My research is inconclusive as to how she interacted with the nursemaid thereafter. However, a pattern seems to appear at the death of each of her children—she believed that it was God's doing to take her children or at least God was using these circumstances to test her heart. She also seemed to feel that God allowed them to be taken because she treasured them above her ministry and calling; that her spiritual focus had not been on heavenly, but on earthly things. This sentiment is echoed in the last paragraph above. The pain of that incident caused her to throw her life into ministry with a new resolve and dedication to seeking God's will alone for her life. This was indicative of the couple's life. Despite their trials and tribulations (sometimes with the church and its leaders) they threw themselves into ministry and did what they were called to do.[23] Phoebe also went on to say that she "resolved not to look at *second causes*,"[24] but take the whole situation as from God directly. I wonder if when she said "second causes," Phoebe meant that she had been pondering as to whether or not she would hold the nursemaid responsible for the death of Eliza. Now that she had resolved the situation as God's will, she was able to be released from her grief and anger.

Phoebe poured all her energy into reaching out to the lost and needy. She founded foster homes for homeless children and fed and clothed the poor. She advocated for anti-slavery laws and women's rights, promoted the work for New York's first rescue mission, and was an officer of the Methodist Ladies' Home Missionary Society. Soon,

22. Wheatley, *Life and Letters of Mrs. Phoebe Palmer*, 31–32.

23. White, *Beauty of Holiness*, 7, 9.

24. Wheatley, *Life and Letters of Mrs. Phoebe Palmer*, 32.

Phoebe became known for her unique way of presenting the gospel. She would go out on the streets, identify the needs, and provide provisions if the individuals or families would attend church. Many came to Christ through her methods.

In 1838 Walter and Phoebe began to travel as Circuit Ministers during the summer months. They almost never missed a year of traveling, except in 1840 when Phoebe almost died from poor health. The couple loved being Circuit Ministers. They started traveling abroad and across the Atlantic, promoting what would be later known as the Holiness Movement.

In 1839 the Palmers had another child named Phoebe, who survived along with their youngest child named Walter Clarke (born in 1843). Little Walter completed their family, at least until 1855.

In 1855 the Palmers were touched by the unusual story of a Jewish boy who had converted to Christianity and was disowned by his family. In a letter to Bishop Leonidas Hamline, dated April 28, 1855, Phoebe wrote:

> Well, we have also, in yet more immediate prospect another dear child. When we come, we hope to have the privilege of introducing you to Leopold Solomon Palmer, our Jewish boy. You will remember that he was thrown into prison for embracing the Christian faith. We expect to receive his indenture tomorrow. He is bound to us by the city authorities. We take him as our *child*, in the name of the Methodist public, to train him for the ministry to which he feels himself called.[25]

The Palmers were granted permission from the city authorities to take him as their own child. They trained him for ministry, because he felt called to it. They sent him off to a "Charlottesville Seminary" (the exact location and full name of the seminary is not known). When he returned home on vacation his natural family persuaded him to return to their faith and family. It was a difficult situation on all sides, but the Palmers were happy to have loved him while they could. Unfortunately, the boy was never heard from again.[26]

---

25. Ibid., 213. It is hard to believe that anyone would be thrown into prison merely for their faith in America during this time period. It would be more likely that Leopold broke a law, or was falsely accused, or perhaps Phoebe was mistaken.

26. Ibid., 634–35.

Not held back by family, the Palmers continued to travel and preach, leaving their children in the hands of capable care givers. Many people enjoyed Phoebe's preaching (although she was never technically a preacher, as she was not licensed). Phoebe told stories to enhance her sermons, as opposed to the traditional form of preaching at that time. In Charles White's book *The Beauty of Holiness*, a woman leaving the Palmers' meeting is quoted as saying "A man has been here, and he preaches, and his wife exhorts, and she is the best of the two."[27] White goes on to suggest that "The woman probably felt that way because Walter preached and Phoebe told stories." He goes on to say, "God reveals his truth to us through 'types, historical narratives, and emblems.' Mrs. Palmer chose to simplify spiritual realities to make 'them tangible to the understanding of the humble' by telling stories."[28] A Canadian minister named the Reverend W. Young described what it was like to be in a service with her:

> As a public speaker, she was unique and peculiar, copying after no one, yet possibly reminding one of Mr. Wesley, whom she so much admired. Deep feeling, intense earnest, love to Christ, and the souls of men, completely annihilating every opposing influence and feeling; cool and deliberate; voice clear, utterance distinct, words carefully considered and well chosen; a perfect model of modesty and confidence. I shall never forget the effect produced on both head and heart, by the first public address I heard her deliver. It was at the first of the above mentioned camp-meetings. About noon, on the Lord's day, she was called upon, without previous notice, at the close of a sermon, to speak to a congregation of several thousands. Curiosity soon gave way to a higher and nobler feeling. Breathless attention was given. Every eye was fixed upon her.
>
> Those in the rear of the congregation, place their hands behind their ears, that not a word might be lost. Before she got through, the Holy Ghost came down and melted many hearts. In the social circle, she was communicative and instructive. Her religion appeared to make her happy and cheerful. It was the constant theme of her conversation, and the great work of her life.[29]

27. White, *Beauty of Holiness*, 173.
28. Ibid.
29. Wheatley, *Life and Letters of Mrs. Phoebe Palmer*, 634–35.

The Palmers first visit to Canada was in 1854 to a camp meeting in a farmer's field in Napanee, Canada West (now Ontario), where the Canadians were especially responsive. During that four-day visit, five hundred people were converted. The Palmers returned again in 1857 (when Walter was 53 years old and Phoebe 50) on a journey in which their travels were even more extensive into the heart of what we know as Ontario today. Most of their ministry that year concentrated in and around Toronto (including the Methodist Victoria College), and was marked with great success—including the worldwide revival that was ignited during their visit to Hamilton.

It was said that Phoebe liked preaching in Canada because Canada was "more primitive" than the United States (meaning less populated and developed, less obstructed by worldly things and more open to the word of God). She noted the landscape of Canada, especially Niagara Falls, using nature itself to speak to her about God's ways. Perhaps she also loved Canada because Canada was ahead of the United States in political issues such as anti-slavery laws and other issues that she regarded as important. In fact, Phoebe sided with anti-slavery laws despite the opposite opinions of some of her friends and colleagues.[30]

After their ministry in 1857, the Palmers returned home. Walter settled into his practice once again; he agreed that Phoebe needed to continue her preaching. Phoebe continued her travels, preaching in five different cities that winter—spreading the news of revival. By the time March 1858 came, Phoebe was preaching inter-denominationally. In the summer of 1858, the couple visited the Canadian Maritimes, spreading the Good News, and leading 21,000 people to receive the justifying and sanctifying grace of God.[31]

Four years of traveling in the British Isles began in 1859 for the couple, as they brought the message of revival along with them. Walter would eventually retire from his medical practice and live off his savings from that successful business while continuing to preach the gospel with his wife.

---

30. Smith, *Revivalism and Social Reform*, 211.
31. White, *Beauty of Holiness*, 238.

THE PALMERS' REVIVAL PRINCIPLES

It is important to understand how the Palmers thought and what they believed, because their trip to Hamilton did not follow their own usual guidelines for accepting an invitation to preach. Here are the general rules they lived by for deciding where they were to go (of course they always went to a place that needed the message of Christ, and also tried to listen to what the Holy Spirit prompted them to do).

The Palmers' Criteria for Accepting Ministry away from Home[32]

1. An official invitation must come their way. It must be urgent and unanimous from both the pastor and the congregation. This would encourage people to pray, not criticize. After seeking what they felt was God's direction for their journey, they would often choose to go to a place of great need, and not the most convenient or popular place.

2. The people must be urged to make a great sacrifice. Phoebe would use the example of what Dr. Palmer did with his medical practice, by giving a portion of his business time to ministry or by providing medicine to those in need at his own expense.

3. The church needs to follow-up. Funds must be given to continue the work.

In *The Beauty of Holiness*, the details of Phoebe's beliefs about revival are outlined. She believed that anyone could be saved at any time. She also believed that God is always eager to visit his people. This theology was the basis for belief that revival could occur at any time.

For Phoebe Palmer then, revival was, "only a return to primitive Christianity untrammelled by mere human opinions and church conventionalisms"; it was "an experimental recognition of the doctrines of heart holiness, or in other words, the full baptism of the Holy Ghost, such as the120 received on the day of Pentecost"; Pentecost itself was the first revival, and because God baptizes with the Spirit today, the church may experience Pentecost today. God has established the plans for revival, and according to Mrs. Palmer, if Christians follow them, there is no reason the revival cannot begin "this hour!" "TRUE REVIVALS ARE

32. Ibid., 171–77.

THE EFFECTS OF A LAW," she declared. All that believers need to do is work according to that law, and they will see "a model revival."[33]

Stages in a Layman's Revival

White also gives the stages that Phoebe outlined for having a layman's revival. Here are the stages:

1. Pastors must be in agreement with holiness doctrine.

2. People must not only seek the knowledge but the experience of salvation and holiness.

3. In order to grow good believers, good strong believers must be able to teach, preach, and pray with the new converts, for God has given brains to the Christians to cheat the devil of his prey. Congregations must be able to help new converts pray if they are having a difficult time, or until they receive their sought-for blessing, and to help unbelievers journey toward having a stronger walk with God.

4. Leaders should interview candidates for their testimony and on various subjects, so that the candidates can begin preaching through the use of their testimonies in interview format.

5. The church needs to follow up with encouragement for new believers and workers, as well as teaching of evangelism through organized efforts and bands of "Christian Vigilance" for soul-winning purposes.[34]

Throughout her writings, Phoebe continued to teach Christians how to keep evangelism in the forefront of their minds. She often appealed to Christians to make this a part of their lives and become accountable to one another by creating Soul-Saver Bands (Groups).

Creating Soul-Saver Bands/Christian Vigilance Bands[35]

These were Phoebe's instructions for the small groups:

1. Make "secular business or domestic avocations specifically subservient to the service of Christ."

2. Spend one half hour daily, or more if possible, "in specific, direct efforts to win souls for Christ." Is there no one around to witness to?

---

33. Ibid., 166.
34. Ibid., 171–77.
35. Palmer, *Promise of the Father*, 262–65. See also White, *Beauty of Holiness*, 175.

Write letters to the unsaved. Tell the unsaved that they are prayed for by name.

3. Do your best to interest other professed Christians, no matter what their denomination, in the task of evangelism.

4. Meet together weekly to pray for each other and report on your progress.

5. Meet monthly with any other bands in the city under the guidance of a minister.

Hamilton Was a Special Case

What I find interesting is that Phoebe and Walter never received an official advance invitation to visit Hamilton. When the circumstances prevented them from further travel, an invitation to participate in the weekly prayer meeting was given. Although the churches may have prepared their people with teaching about revival, revival was not expected. As you will see, Phoebe stayed true to her methods of evangelism and revival, and the local preachers were to remain on in Hamilton and encourage the practice of a revival by creating bands or groups of people to continue the work after she left.

Now that we have examined an overview of the theology and strategy driving Phoebe's revivals, we will delve into the story of the Hamilton Revival and how it links in with the Second Great Awakening.

6

The Humble Origins of a Great Awakening

AMIDST THE DIFFICULTIES THAT Hamilton and the world were experiencing, biblically inspired Christians believed that God still
wanted to bless those who sought him. Evangelists, missionaries, revivalists, and preachers reached out to those who had left the fold, to
those whose faith had grown cold, and to those who did not have a living
relationship with God. They encouraged ordinary Christians to do the
same. Already in place were the ministers of Hamilton who knew about
revival and the move of God from other times, and who could minister
to the laity effectively. The next step was to bring the Palmers who would
begin a revival in Hamilton.

FOILED PLANS, OCTOBER 8, 1857

On October 8, 1857, Phoebe and Walter Palmer had finished their last
camp meeting for the season in Oakville, Ontario. They had had a good
summer with what they considered great camp meetings in Nova Scotia,
New Brunswick, and Prince Edward Island, with large attendance and
good response to what they believed to be the movement of the Holy
Spirit.[1] At the close of the Oakville camp meeting they began their journey home, going by train with a few other circuit ministers to Hamilton,
where the company was to split up and go their separate ways. Originally
their plan was to stay just a few hours in Hamilton and continue their

---

1. Semple, *The Lord's Dominion*, 142. This is the only place where Semple acknowledges the 1857 revival in Hamilton. He states: "The Palmers also held large revivals
in Hamilton, Oakville, and Toronto." He continues on to say, "The publicity from this
triumphant crusade has been credited with inspiring a massive revival in the United
States and Britain the following year, although revivals had been taking place in New
England during 1857."

journey homeward across Lake Ontario via the Albany boat. In a letter to her sister Sarah Lankford, dated October 10, 1857, Phoebe explains what happened that night:

> We arrived at Hamilton about dark, and Dr. P. made an effort to check his baggage through for Friday, so as to reach home by the Albany boat on Saturday morning. But God has, in a wonderful manner, detained us at every step. Dr. P. was frustrated in his attempt to leave his baggage, and we went to the house of a friend, to remain over night, intending to leave for home early in the morning. It was the usual evening for prayer-meeting in the three churches here. Two of the ministers received information of our unexpected visit, and before we had finished our tea, were with us. They immediately made arrangements for uniting the prayer-meetings.[2]

It is unclear exactly what role the trains played in keeping the Palmers in Hamilton, but they did play a part. It is important to note that even the delays were considered a divine intervention by Phoebe, as she stated in a letter written from Hamilton on October 17, 1857: "We were on our way homeward from one of the most glorious meetings we ever attended; and had the railroad cars favoured our purpose, we should have been with our New York friends one week yesterday."[3]

Phoebe had a philosophy, which she wrote about when explaining the incident to a friend: "you would be assured that your disappointment is God's appointment."[4] So, in keeping with her nature, she remained connected with God, despite her circumstances, and made arrangements to stay the night at a friend's home in Hamilton. A similar sentiment of her belief in divine intervention is shown in the letter below, written most likely in December of that same year.

> MY BELOVED SISTER T.—How little did I think, when parting with you on the Oakville camp-ground, that we should have lingered in those regions till this time. We paused here on the evening of the day we left you with the expectation of tarrying but for the night. But the Angel of the Covenant in the infinitude of His love and wisdom has withstood us in our homeward progress thus far.[5]

2. Wheatley, *Life and Letters of Mrs. Phoebe Palmer*, 328–29.

3. Palmer, *Promise of the Father*, 251–52.

4. Wheatley, *Life and Letters of Mrs. Phoebe Palmer*, 330.

5. Palmer, "A Revival after Apostolic Times."

After being stranded in Hamilton, it would appear that Phoebe remained open to a new plan.

AN INVITATION

Reverend Samuel Rice heard of the Palmers' delay in traveling, and was excited that they were staying in Hamilton for the night. While attending the Oakville camp meeting, he had tried to encourage the Palmers to visit Hamilton. In an article reporting the events to *The Christian Guardian*, Samuel Rice writes the following:

> While at the meeting I had invited Dr. and Mrs. Palmer to pay me a visit, but absence from home at several of our autumn camp-meetings had been so protracted that they deferred the acceptance of the invitation to a future time; but under a guidance divine at the point of separation, they decided to stay a little with us, and on Thursday evening they came to our city in company with several from the Camp-ground. The design was formed to test the principle of a "laity for the times." Each of us took a short ramble, as we could find to meet with the Dr. and Mrs. Palmer at the Mc Nab-street [*sic*] church. This was our starting point.[6]

Excited that the Palmers were in town, Rev. Rice took a short ramble to the MacNab Street church most likely from King and Wellington (the site of the King Street church) or from John and Gore (the site of the John Street church). There he met with the Palmers as they finished their afternoon tea.

Since it was the regular night for the Hamilton Wesleyan Methodist churches' prayer meeting, a request was made that all three churches join together in prayer. The ministers agreed to open the John Street Church as the central location because it had a lecture room in the basement that was perfect for the prayer meeting.[7]

NEW PLANS

As the Palmers and the three ministers walked to gather at the John Street Church, Phoebe felt prompted by what she felt was the Holy Spirit. She described the Holy Spirit's prompting that continued on into the meeting:

6. Rice,"The Work of God in Hamilton."
7. Wheatley, *Life and Letters of Mrs. Phoebe Palmer*, 330.

As we proceeded to the meeting, the Spirit of the Lord urged the test, "Call upon me and I will answer thee, and show thee great and mighty things, things that thou knewest [*sic*] not." And while talking in the meeting, I felt a Divine power pressing me mightily to urge upon the people to set themselves apart at once, to work for God in promoting a revival. I felt the Holy Spirit working in my own heart powerfully, and assured the people if they would at once "bring all the tithes into the Lord's store house," and prove Him therewith, that He would open the windows of heaven and pour out such a blessing as would overflow the regions round about, and result in hundreds on hundreds being brought home to God.[8]

So Phoebe followed the leading of the Spirit. The results were as follows:

It was the stated prayer meeting evening, and about seventy persons were present. We were led to speak of the solemn obligation of bringing *all* the tithes into the Lord's storehouse, in order that all the tithes of time, talent, and estate might be laid on God's holy altar, and thus be brought into immediate use, by way of saving a lost world. We suggested that if the people would pledge themselves thus to bring all the Lord's tithes into his storehouse at once, and go to work on the morrow to invite their neighbours to Christ, gracious results might be seen the ensuing evening. Probably over thirty of those present raised their right hand in the presence of the Lord, in solemn affirmation that they would sacrifice that which cost them something, in earnest, specific endeavors to win souls to Christ.[9]

After the initial prayer meeting concluded, Phoebe noted her feelings, despite the promptings of the Spirit. "When we paused on our journey here, on Thursday last, one week since, with the expectation of tarrying but for the night, there was nothing in the tone of the meeting we attended which indicated the near approach of this extraordinary outpouring of the Spirit."[10]

Rev. Rice also described the initial prayer meeting and unfolding events. It would seem as though outwardly nothing out of the ordinary was about to happen.

8. Ibid., 329.
9. Palmer, *Promise of the Father*, 254–55.
10. Ibid., 254.

There was a good attendance for the notice. Mrs. Palmer in her lucid and pointed manner, under such feelings as the Holy Spirit alone can produce, placed her thoughts before the company assembled—gave us an outline of a plan for personal effort, in the form of a home "camp-meeting," stating the state of heart necessary to engage successfully in such an enterprise. After stating the plan of personal effort clearly, time was given for consideration, and then each one willing to work was requested to give in his adhesion to the plan by rising. Most of those present arose and then came forward for special prayer for divine power and direction.[11]

There was very little emotion during the meeting that night, unlike the emotions that had marked many revivals prior, which has fascinated many scholars today. Phoebe was obedient in sharing what God had laid on her heart from Malachi 3—to share our tithes of money, time, and talent, in essence, every aspect of our lives. One of Phoebe's letters indicates that when she shared what God had laid on her heart from Malachi 3, she spoke of surrendering every aspect of one's life, including surrender of the reputation.[12] There were Christians who understood this as a call to lay down what was considered reputable (marks of status) in the world, if necessary, in order to obey God. They believed that the results of obeying God would outweigh the choice to please human beings, as noted in the attitude and actions of the mayor of Hamilton, as described later in this chapter.

She then challenged the people to commit to move out of their comfort zone. Her husband, Walter, closed off the meeting that night of October 8, 1857.

Between sixty and seventy people showed up for that initial prayer meeting out of the approximately 500 members of the three Wesleyan churches.[13] They were challenged to believe and pray for a revival similar to what they knew from attending camp meetings. As Phoebe further wrote about the events of that night, "Thirty, perhaps, or more of those present lifted their hand in the solemn presence of God that they would begin to work *immediately*."[14] Later Phoebe would realize that this was a

11. Rice, "The Work of God in Hamilton."
12. Wheatley, *Life and Letters of Mrs. Phoebe Palmer*, 329.
13. Ibid., 330.
14. Ibid.

turning point, and would state, "Thus it was that the battle was at once, in the most unlooked-for manner, pushed to the gate."[15]

Phoebe Palmer shared how, that evening, after the initial prayer meeting and upon prayer and reflection, she spent the night in communication with God. "During the night, my spirit was awake with God, much of the time, and I received a divine conviction that God was about to bring out people in multitudes and stamp our ideas of a 'laity for the times,' with signal success."[16]

Phoebe would soon see if what her spirit was receiving was indeed a word from God.

THE NEXT EVENING—OCTOBER 9, 1857

Believing that God wanted to do something big, the Palmers and the Hamilton ministers gathered together to discuss what the next steps were.

> A special meeting was appointed for the next evening. Each one had obligated himself to bring at least one with him, and to invite as many as possible. On coming together in the evening, the lecture room was found wholly insufficient to contain the people, and the large audience room was resorted to.[17]

> The minister stationed here felt in the same way, on all sides it was agreed that the body of the large and most central church had better be opened. Hundreds came out, though it was not the usual meeting night, and nothing was known of the meeting, only as the gospel invitations had spread rapidly from one to another, to come out and seek salvation.[18]

The leadership at the John Street church would encourage the participants to move the meeting from the lecture room to the sanctuary to accommodate the larger numbers. It was a good thing that they were unified in this move, for they would soon discover that God was about to do a great thing.[19]

15. Ibid.
16. Ibid.
17. Palmer, "A Revival after Apostolic Times."
18. Wheatley, *Life and Letters of Mrs. Mrs. Phoebe Palmer*, 330.
19. Ibid.

Phoebe, encouraged by the large attendance and the twenty-one converts, decided to stay on in Hamilton until the work was established. She describes the second meeting's impact:

> The invitation for seekers of salvation to come to the altar, had not been given more than five minutes, I think, before the altar was crowded. Before the meeting closed, twenty-one earnest seeking penitents were rejoicing in God. The most, or all of these, were persons gathered in from the world, and brought to the house of God by the urgent solicitations of those who lifted their hand to work for God, the evening previous. You will not wonder that we dared not leave now. [20]

Phoebe describes the events below as every pastor's dream: the people had listened and taken action, following their pastors' lead.

> Ministers had been alike diligent as the laity in giving sinners a personal invitation to come to Christ. The invitation had been accepted, and the glorious result of the first day's effort was that a score of souls were added to the ranks of the saved. And now the newly saved were pledged, in turn, to unite with those already in the field, in bringing their unsaved friends to Jesus. A meeting was appointed for the next afternoon and evening, and still the number doubled and [tripled] until hundreds are now in daily attendance in the afternoon and evening meetings, and the revival seems to be the absorbing topic of all circles. And who can say where it will end? Think of the three or four hundred new recruits, and these all engaged alike with those before in the field, in daily renewal of efforts to bring one more.[21]

Christians began with renewed vigor to share their faith, and step out of their normal way of conducting their life, and expecting God to move. As a result, revival began to break out as new converts came to Christ, and in the days and weeks to follow the numbers grew exponentially.

Rev. Samuel Rice described to the Canadian Methodist Newspaper, *The Christian Guardian*, the agreed outline the Palmers and the ministers used to promote the work of the Holy Spirit in Hamilton:

> The plan of conducting the meetings was simple; one of ourselves stationed on the circuit opened the meeting and gave a short ad-

20. Ibid.
21. Palmer, *Promise of the Father*, 255.

dress. Mrs. Palmer followed, and Dr. Palmer invited seekers of salvation forward, while those who had been busy inviting persons during the day, looked after such in the meeting; thus all were at work, either in the prayer circle or in the congregation in true camp-meeting fashion.[22]

Thus the spontaneous Hamilton protracted meetings were in motion. The revival meetings flourished in the colder Canadian weather, and the church provided a dedicated place without distraction for those seeking God. The meeting's schedule allotted time for working people to continue their responsibilities.

THE DAYS FOLLOWING IN HAMILTON—APPROXIMATELY OCTOBER 10–18, 1857

Rev. Rice eloquently summed up what happened after the initial prayer meeting and in the days that followed:

> God that night, accepted the sincerely offered devotion of his children's heart and labour, and from that private meeting, those who had pledged themselves for labour, went forth to fulfill their vows and redeem their pledges. The result was immediate. Attention to the great subject of personal salvation became apparent and scores night after night, presented themselves for prayer, and professed salvation.[23]

Phoebe wrote in the days following the events how the revival grew. "Nightly we pledged ourselves anew to bring yet one more the coming day; and thus the hosts of Zion are enlarging daily, and new cases are being ferreted out, which would never have been reached but by this system of vigorous daily effort."[24] She continued in another letter:

> We had but one very short sermon, during the whole week. One of the ministers would generally say a few introductory stirring words, and then leave the meeting with ourselves, to follow up the remarks. Dr. P.'s prayer-meeting tact is of course brought into constant requisition, to bring up the rear.[25]

22. Rice, "The Work of God in Hamilton."
23. Ibid.
24. Palmer, "A Revival after Apostolic Times."
25. Wheatley, *Life and Letters of Mrs. Phoebe Palmer*, 331.

In a letter dated October 14, 1857, to her sister Sarah Lankford, Phoebe wrote:

> One week ago to-day, such a work commenced in Hamilton, as has never been witnessed before. Between one and two hundred have been translated out of the kingdom of darkness into the kingdom of God's dear Son. Last night, forty-five were saved; the evening previous, thirty, and the evenings previous, about twenty each evening.
>
> Such a Sabbath as yesterday, we never saw. Meetings were being held from seven o'clock in the morning till ten in the evening, in all of which I believe some were saved. We have had but very little preaching. I mean preaching in the technical sense, according to the idea of preaching in the present day. And though I would not be understood to speak lightly of the value of well beaten oil for the service of the sanctuary, yet never have I been so confirmed in a belief long since adopted, in regard to the sort of preaching in the present day. It is the preaching of apostolic times, when all the church membership were "scattered throughout the regions of Judea and Samaria, *except* the apostles." And these scattered bands, of newly baptized disciples, though so young in the faith, and composed of men, women, and children, went everywhere preaching the Word. Surely, dear Sister Sarah, this, in the most empathetic sense, is the sort of preaching which has been made instrumental in this great revival.[26]

According to the Rev. Rice, the ministers agreed that they needed to continue in their plans to promote the movement of the Holy Spirit. It worked. The growth of the church continued; those in attendance were discipled and supported by those who labored in prayer.

Rev. Rice wrote:

> Monday evenings are given to the subject of Holiness, each minister on the circuit in his turn presiding. These meetings are more largely attended and possess a larger measure of divine power than any other of our week evening services. The number of our praying labouring band is increased, and not a week passes without the conversion or restoration of souls.[27]

---

26. Ibid., 330–31. Phoebe might have meant that the work commenced in "such a manner that has never been witnessed before" in Hamilton.

27. Rice, "The Work of God in Hamilton."

The historian J. Edwin Orr writes, "What followed was utterly unplanned and unprogrammed, observers attributing the event to the work of the Holy Spirit."[28]

For the next four weeks, following the initial meeting (comprised of people from the three Wesleyan churches), only one short sermon was preached for twenty minutes. The rest of the time lay people (the non-ordained) gave testimony to what God had done—and they believed they had seen God's Spirit move mightily. Just one Thursday night message, spoken to a crowd of between sixty and seventy (possibly comprised of people from the three attending churches), with just over thirty people committing to do the work of God, produced a harvest that was truly inspiring. It would seem as though God had prepared the people of Hamilton for Phoebe's message to render their time, possessions, and selves to God. The leaders continued to give up their agendas and allow for what they believed were the heart promptings of the Holy Spirit to oversee and conduct the plans of the meetings.

This is the breakdown of the Hamilton revival results: Twenty-one converts came to Christ the day after the initial meeting (Friday), and then two meetings were held on Saturday with over twenty and then forty-five professing salvation, ending the week with Sunday's two meetings and salvations between twenty and thirty each meeting. The result, as stated in Phoebe's letter to her sister Sarah of October 14th, was over one hundred souls in three days. In that same letter, the count for the week was three hundred to four hundred salvations, but a post-script reveals that, as she was finishing the letter, Phoebe heard that the salvation count was up to five hundred. By the end of their eighteen-day stay, Phoebe and Walter witnessed five hundred new conversions. In other words: ten days plus one formal sermon and four weeks of revival, plus the two further weeks of meetings yielded six hundred converts, truly a remarkable event in those days.[29] The evidence suggests that the leadership and the laity had heard from God.[30]

28. Orr and Roberts, *Event of the Century*, 26.

29. How the revival progressed for two more weeks after the Palmers left is discussed in chapter 8, "What Happened Next in Hamilton," and in Rice's letter, "The Work of God in Hamilton."

30. Wheatley, *Life and Letters of Mrs. Phoebe Palmer*, 330. See also Palmer, *Promise of the Father*. Phoebe's account of the numbers saved is not always consistent. Increases may be due to more people's decisions having been documented or coming to light in days following. It is important to note that this was a count of the newly converted, and

As Phoebe noted, "One of the ministers, speaking of this since, said, 'The battle was set in array so suddenly, that Satan himself had not time to contemplate a defence.'"[31] It surely was unplanned, unprogrammed, and unexpected by all, except God.

Phoebe understood the challenges revival brought and expressed her appreciation for the ministers who worked in unity with the Spirit. She also reveled in the Christians' ability to respond and carry out the work God had blessed them with.

> Though Hamilton is favored with three devoted ministers, than whom few are more marked, in our own or any other church, for eminent devotedness and ministerial ability, yet these ministers will be as free to acknowledge, to the praise of God, as ourselves, that this gust of divine power, now spreading as a pentecostal flame over this entire community, took its rise in the sudden rise of the *laity*.[32]

Phoebe would also say,

> Though few churches can boast of such ministers for talent and devotedness, and we are earnest in our acknowledgements that as shepherds of this newly gathered flock, their care and also affectionate teachings and guidance, are *absolutely* needful, yet we again say, that though favored with the constant aid of their three resident ministers, and other ministers, visitors of high position, district chairmen, etc.—yet this revival took its rise mainly with the laity. It did not commence in laborious pulpit effort, neither has it progressed in this way.[33]

---

did not include those who received entire sanctification or the filling of the Holy Spirit (as noted in chapter 3). In her letter dated October 26th in the *Christian Guardian*, Phoebe notes that the "above estimate [of 300–400 converts] is probably below the actual number, as many names, especially of those who received entire sanctification were not recorded." I am not sure why Phoebe returned to the figure 300–400 in this letter, written after the other. Perhaps it was to be modest. Some documents state that the revival took place over six weeks. My research shows that the Palmers stayed for a little over two weeks in Hamilton, and the meetings continued for about ten more days after they left (or perhaps more, the documents are inconclusive). The six weeks given by some writers may include the additional time spent in London, Ontario; however, if that is included, the number of converts should include the 200 who were saved there as well. Samuel Rice, "the Work of God in Hamilton" talks of having a record of 600 names of persons newly converted in the revival. This was written after the Palmers had left.

31. Wheatley, *Life and Letters of Mrs. Phoebe Palmer*, 329.

32. Palmer, *Promise of the Father*, 253–54.

33. Wheatley, *Life and Letters of Mrs. Phoebe Palmer*, 331.

The evidence indicates that it absolutely was a layman's revival and the ministers had facilitated the move of God. The people's obedience to what they believed to be the Holy Spirit's moving made it easier for the ministers, as they were not the center of attention, and the converted were being raised up to participate in the Great Commission (Matthew 28:16–20).

ACCOUNTS, WITNESSES, TESTIMONIES, AND SPREAD OF THE REVIVAL

Soon all of Hamilton and the surrounding areas were buzzing with the news of what was happening. The following are recorded excerpts and documentation of the spreading revival. As people took a bold, potentially new and scary step for God, they found that evangelism wasn't a strange or uncomfortable thing. Speaking about their relationship with Christ began to flow out of who they were. They were able to maintain their friendships and reputation with those who did not know God. They quickly came to believe that if they did the work of evangelism, they could trust God for the results.

Mr. Rice noted the unusual facts about the revival: "The peculiar characteristic of the work was the ease and rapidity with which it moved. There was a great absence of external manifestations; the emotions were usually entirely under the control of the subjects of this work. I state this as a fact, not thereby expressing an opinion as to whether it was better or worse on this account."[34]

In a newspaper article, Phoebe describes the fervor with which this revival spread. While Phoebe was still in Hamilton, people started to travel from afar to come, see, and experience what was happening there. I imagine that the same fervor continued for a while afterwards. The ministers from other areas were bearing witness to the authenticity of the revival, and were most likely receiving a blessing themselves, and probably hoped that they could duplicate such a blessing for both the Christians and non-Christians in their own churches and community. Sadly, I was not able to identify who these ministers from surrounding stations were. Although, as previously noted, they probably weren't from the Methodist Episcopal Church or the Free Union Church, it would be nice to imagine for ecumenical reasons that some of these ministers

34. Rice, "The Work of God in Hamilton."

would be from outside of the Wesleyan Methodist tradition. Phoebe went on to say the following:

> I saw a man and his wife to-day who had come seventy-five miles expressly in view of coming to the meeting, and sharing in the shower of grace now falling. They came hungering and thirsting after righteousness, and returned this morning to their home, filled with the joys of a full salvation, to spread, we trust the holy flame in their own region. Three or four Ministers also, from the surrounding stations have received the witness of Holiness, whose faith, we trust many of their people may be induced to follow. Instances of exceeding interest come crowding upon my mind, the narration of which would, I am sure call forth the burst of praise from your ever attuned lips: but here my pen must pause; opportunity fails. We must leave for London to-day, having given the friends some encouragement to expect us, in answer to an earnest invitation to spend a short time with them.[35]

In another letter, Phoebe detailed some of the encounters she had with both Christians and non-Christians during her stay. As the revival built momentum, it seems that everyday Christians, and not just the professional clergy and evangelists, were bringing the message of salvation to the unsaved. The message of salvation spoken by ordinary Christians brought a profound conviction to the ones seemingly furthest away from God. I think it probably surprised the laity when they stepped out, and realized that they too could have a great impact. The leadership involved believed that God was using these ordinary Christians led by the Spirit to evangelize. Sometimes unbelievers needed multiple encounters with Christians to get their attention. People from all walks of life were becoming engaged in the revival, often to the surprise of the leaders. Phoebe wrote another account of this:

> "Wonderful!" exclaimed one of aristocratic bearing, who had long been unapproachable on the subject of his soul's best interest. And now he had been approached by one who, having newly received the baptism of fire, feared to let him alone. The lady, who now dared to meet him in his own home, was one among the many scores who, with uplifted hand, was daily pledging herself to be "instant in season and out of season" in searching out some new subject for Christ's kingdom; and now, on being thus personally addressed, and beholding the tears of earnestness

35. Palmer, "A Revival after Apostolic Times."

streaming from the eyes of the lady addressing him, he exclaimed with amazement, "Wonderful! What can this mean? Never did I see anything like it!" He listened with interest to expostulating tones of pious entreaty as they fell from the lips of the lady, and though he has not yielded to the claims of Christ, he has had a season of the Spirit's visitation, through human agency, without which the church might not have been clear of his blood, should he be lost.

Said another, who was a lady of some position, but who had long been a neglecter of salvation, "Why here is more than half a dozen different persons who have to-day been running to me on this subject. I do not see what has got into the people. Why, they must think that I am a dreadful sinner."

All classes are at work. Illustrations of exceeding interest come up before me; but I can scarcely trust myself to glance at them, they are so numerous and so suggestive. Seldom have I seen a more lovely convert than one in the common walks of life. After her translation from the kingdom of darkness into the kingdom of God's dear Son, she was so entranced with the glory of the inheritance upon which she had just entered, that the utterances of her new-born Spirit were singularly beautiful and sublime. I mentioned this on my return to the family where we were entertained. "O, that is the one our Eliza brought," said our hostess. Eliza is a pious servant in the family, but, though pressed with an unusual amount of service just at this time, she had with others, lifted her hand by way of pledging herself to bring at least one.

"I did not know that our servant knew a person in the place, as we brought her from a distance, not very long since; but she had pledged herself to bring one, and that one was converted." So said the Rev. Mr. R., the minister who superintends the work here. The work is becoming the town topic. Men of business are after men of business; every man after his man. Surely this is a truthful demonstration of Christianity in earnest, and a return to what was said by an eminent divine of the more early Methodists—"They are all at it, and always at it."[36]

What caught the attention of on-lookers was not only the mass of converts of all ages and walks of life, but the godly mayor of Hamilton, John Francis Moore, who was seen participating in prayer. He was spotted at the altar next to humble servants, mixing with all classes; an un-

36. Palmer, *Promise of the Father*, 257.

usual sight as social classes did not traditionally participate together in communal events.

1857 Mayor of Hamilton, John Francis Moore

> Thanks to the Lord of the harvest for such an in-gathering. And where will it end? Not, we trust, till all Canada is in a blaze. The work is taking within its range persons of all classes. Men of low degree, and men of high estate for wealth and position, old men and maidens, and even little children, are seen humbly kneeling together, pleading for grace. The mayor of the city, with other persons of like position are not ashamed to be seen bowed at the altar of prayer beside the humble servant, pleading for the full baptism of the Spirit.[37]

This was an exciting time for the Christian church in Hamilton. The reports show that many came to profess their love for Christ and their lives changed for the better, by Christ's love and teachings. This encouraged the Christians, who began to act out their faith by going against the social barriers that society and not God had erected. The results of this were demonstrated when humanly built barriers between social classes,

37. Ibid., 252–53.

races, and genders were no longer adhered too, as they alienated God's children from each other. For the Wesleyan tradition, holiness was not only a social concept, but was also deeply personal, and these barriers should not exist; therefore the Hamilton Christians were aligned with their church, and more importantly the Bible. Rev. Rice noted how the Christians were strengthened by this move, and were acting out their faith with results in the following remark:

> During the progress of the work which marked so many as "justified," a large number sought and found that "perfect love that casteth out fear," and are now "walking in the fear of the Lord and comfort of the Holy Ghost." These are numbered by scores, and clearly witnessed by a holy life that "the blood of Jesus Christ His Son, cleanseth them from all sin."[38]

It is also apparent from the documents that the focus of the revival in Hamilton for the leaders was not about which church was the best to attend; it was purely about salvation and holiness—the setting of lives apart for God. This is the true spirit of revival. Rev. Rice wrote a brief description of the nature of the revival meetings that drew people from different walks of life, denominations, and areas giving participants hope and courage:

> The Dr. and Mrs. Palmer remained with us a little over a fortnight after, and in that time and a fortnight after over 600 names were entered on our registry as saved. Some of those had been in the church; some were members—some from the country, and many from other churches in the city, for our meetings were not for proselytism but for salvations, and I doubt not that the registration was in the main a fair index of the results of four week's campaign.[39]

Despite the count in the index, the meetings did grow and did attract some people that had already been Christians for some time, but they also gained new Christians.[40] Soon afterwards Centenary Methodist

---

38. Rice, "The Work of God in Hamilton."

39. Ibid. See also the section above on Hamilton churches.

40. Phoebe's writings often speak about how many new Christians were added to the churches in the revival, but also how many existing Christians were strengthened in their walk, with what most likely she believed to be their acceptance of entire sanctification.

Church (later known as Centenary United) would be built to accommodate the overflow of the new converts.

It was acknowledged by Phoebe that Hamilton was birthing a great move of God. Phoebe recorded these Hamilton events in a letter to her sister Sarah. She specified that if the events would encourage the saints, that they should be shared. "If you think the contents of this letter would interest the attendants on the Tuesday meeting, you are at liberty either to read it, or to relate such portions of it as you think redound to the *glory of God.*"[41]

In Mrs. E. A. Boice's obituary, posted under the title "The Righteous Dead" in the August 6, 1890 issue of *The Christian Guardian*, there is a small reference to her being a part of the 1857 Hamilton Revival. Although the writer of the obituary may have gotten the date wrong, there is no mistake that Mrs. E. A. Boice was a part of the 1857 Hamilton Revival. In fact, she had the opportunity to host the Palmers.

> In October 1859, she was instrumental in inducing the well-known and devoted evangelists, Dr. and Mrs. Palmer, to remain in Hamilton for two weeks as her guests, during which time a memorable work of grace broke out in the city, which added largely to the membership of the three churches . . . The memory of this time of blessing was always a source of great comfort and delight to Mrs. Boice.[42]

The obituary goes on to describe Mrs. Boice as caring for others and overcoming obstacles in her life, like her husband's paralysis. It implies that her faith in God, her position and connections to the Hamilton churches, her experiences with revivalists, and a revival was what gave her strength to continue. You can read her obituary in the Appendix.

I am unable to conclude at this point whether the Palmers were staying with Mrs. Boice in her home. We do know that they were her guests at her church, and she had contact with them, and was touched deeply by their stay.

So exciting was the news of the Hamilton Revival that it was posted and circulated in the November 5, 1857 edition of the Methodist *Christian Advocate and Journal* of New York, with a prominent headline "Revival Extraordinary" on its front page, with a sub-title that declared

---

41. Wheatley, *Life and Letters of Mrs. Phoebe Palmer*, 332.

42. "Righteous Dead."

that from three to four hundred souls had been saved in a few days.[43] As men and women around the world heard about the revival, it would appear that they desired one as well. As Christians began to call out to God, and reach out to those around them, all evidence points to the spread of the revival. The revivals in turn would become a part of a greater awakening, helping many to find God in a world that seemed desperate and lost. It does not come as too much of a surprise that as the Palmers left Hamilton, the news of the revival that they carried with them spread and caught the attention and hearts of men and women around them.

LEAVING HAMILTON AND VISITING LONDON

Eventually the Palmers needed to return home to their family and Walter's practice, but first a visit to one more city was necessary. Phoebe recounted in a letter dated November 13, 1857 to the Bishop and Mrs. Hamline what happened when the Palmers left Hamilton and continued their journey to London, Ontario, and then homeward.

> We went from Hamilton to London, because we dared not do otherwise. The London friends having *claims* on us in a way which I cannot now take time to state. We thought we could not remain, as Dr. P's business seemed so peremptorily calling him home. But the Lord soon began to work in London, much as in Hamilton, and when we tore ourselves away from London, at midnight, after remaining twelve days, the number of the newly saved amounted to about two hundred. We left amid a scene of power, and we trust that the work is still going on, but of this we have not had time to hear, since our return. I need not add the work of entire sanctification has also been going on gloriously, at all of their meetings. Hundreds have received the baptism of the Holy Ghost. Never have we had so much occasion to feel that we are immortal till our work is done.[44]

On that same day, Phoebe wrote another letter to Rev. Mr. R—, about having to leave London, Ontario on October 30, 1857.[45] The

43. Again, I think the number 300–400 is a modest accounting, or includes only the early days of the revival.

44. Wheatley, *Life and Letters of Mrs. Phoebe Palmer*, 332–33.

45. It was common in the nineteenth century to refer to people in correspondence by using an initial rather than a name. Based upon the contents of this letter, and the involvement that Rev. Rice had with the revival, I believe that this letter was probably written by Phoebe to Rev. Rice.

Christians there had caught wind of what had happened in Hamilton, and continued the work of the revival. It seems it was a challenge for the Palmers to be torn away from this beautiful move of God.

> New York, November 13, 1857
>
> To Rev. Mr. R—.
>
> Dear Brother: It was near the midnight hour of October 30 that we parted with our London friends. Several brethren and sisters, dearly beloved in the Lord, accompanied us to the cars. There, at that affecting, solemn hour, we strengthened each other's hands in the Lord. Here, at the dead of night, we lingered at the depot about one hour, awaiting the "lightning train," which was to bear us to our distant home. We improved this hour of waiting in proposing plans for future conquests, which we hope may be as unending as eternity for good. As a company of God's sacramental hosts, we had just left a scene of triumph; and here, at this quiet hour, while the world was sleeping around us, we devised ways and means by which we might win the greatest possible number of souls to the Saviour. And here the whole company formed themselves into a band, which might be designated as a *"Soul-saving Band."* The company consisted of male and female followers of the Saviour. Some of these, though lovely and devoted, were timid and comparatively uninitiated in the arts of holy warfare. Others had, during the twelve days' campaign through which we had passed, endured hardness as good soldiers. Many scores, during the twelve days we had labored together in the city of L., enlisted under the Captain of our salvation; and now, as we were about parting, we memorialized the solemn hour by forming ourselves into a band, which we pray, may ever be signalized in the eye of God and man as a band of soul-savers.[46]

She went on to say, "And if the matter is of God, I trust many of our dear Hamilton friends will be induced to form themselves into the bands for this glorious purpose."[47]

Two hundred more souls claimed for the Kingdom in London! That was just the beginning. The Christians in London had committed to Soul Saving Bands (Groups) to continue the work. Phoebe had given guidelines to a structure to continue the work, but she stressed that what was really important was that the believers continued to hear from God

---

46. Palmer, *Promise of the Father*, 261–62.
47. Ibid., 262.

for themselves, to continue to work and not be stuck to a structure, and to always do what God wanted them to do, in the way he wanted it done. So exciting was the work that the Palmers stayed for twelve days, as long as they could, before they had to leave on the midnight train to return home. Bush says, "They stayed in Hamilton for two weeks which was three times longer than their usual stay in a single location."[48]

Now that we have understood what occurred in Hamilton and London, let's uncover how the Hamilton Revival ties into the start of the Second Great Awakening, with far-reaching effects.

48. Bush, "James Caughey, Phoebe and Walter Palmer," 130.

7

The Momentum around the World

THE UNITED STATES: NEW YORK CITY

A LREADY IN PLACE SINCE September 23, 1857 was the New York Union Prayer Meeting, held at the North Church of the Dutch Reformed. It was located at the northwest corner of William Street and Fulton in lower Manhattan's business district—the heart of New York City. The church stood two blocks east of where the World Trade Center stands today, and is now called the Collegiate Reformed Protestant Dutch Church.[1] The New York Union Prayer meetings at the North Church of the Dutch Reformed were headed by Jeremiah Calvin Lanphier, who had been converted at Charles G. Finney's Broadway Tabernacle.[2] Lanphier came to New York with a background in mercantile pursuits, so it would seem natural for him to reach out to businessmen during this time.[3] He passed out pamphlets around the city stating:

> This meeting is intended to give merchants, mechanics, clerks, strangers, and business-men generally, an opportunity to stop and call upon God amid the perplexities incident to their respective avocations. It will continue for one hour; but it is also designed for those who may find it inconvenient to remain more than 5 or 10 minutes, as well as for those who can spare a whole hour.[4]

1. Gray, "Streetscapes."

2. Orr and Roberts, *Event of the Century*, 5. See also Orr, *Second Evangelical Awakening*, 10.

3. Prime, *Power of Prayer*, 20–21.

4. Orr and Roberts, *Event of the Century*, 53–54.

The first meetings were very small with ten people praying; however, by the third meeting (October 7, 1857) forty people came to pray.[5] The fourth meeting (October 8) was one "of uncommon fervency in prayer, of deep humility and self-abasement and great desire that God would glorify himself in the outpouring of his Spirit upon them."[6] The crowds would slowly grow until the bank collapse actually affected New York. On October 14th Lanphier's diary would record the change in the crowd attending the prayer meeting, most likely due to the financial panic that had begun to sweep New York. "Attended the noon-day prayer meeting. Over one hundred present, many of them not professors of religion, but under the conviction of sin, and seeking an interest in Christ; inquiring of what they shall do to be saved. God grant that they find Christ precious to their souls."[7] That day was the turning point for the meeting. It now became the Fulton Street prayer meeting.

Prayer meetings started popping up all over New York. The atmosphere surrounding the meetings is described by Prime. "The place of prayer was a most delightful resort, and places of prayer multiplied because men were moved to prayer. They wished to pray. They felt impelled, by some unseen power to pray. They felt the pressure of the call to prayer."[8] In fact, he goes on to note that evangelism was beginning to happen in these prayer meetings. "The question was never asked, "to what church does he belong?" But the question was, "does he belong to Christ?"[9] By November and December of 1857, Prime says that prayer meetings were not just popping up all over the city, but the land. Much like the Hamilton revival, the atmosphere for this revival was unusual in the way it was uncharacteristically solemn with deeply affected audiences.[10]

By the end of six months (March 1858) ten thousand were in attendance, and more venues were required for prayer meetings.[11] It is important to note that people were drawn to pray, which is the beginning of a

5. Prime, *Power of Prayer*, 23.

6. Ibid., 24.

7. Ibid., 25.

8. Ibid., 27.

9. Ibid.

10. Ibid., 34.

11. Orr, *Second Evangelical Awakening*, 11. See also the section below on the Bank Collapse.

revival or awakening among Christians. However, it is important to note also that in Hamilton, by October 9, 1857, people were being converted to Christ, and it was taken as a sign of revival and the beginning of an awakening for both Christians and non-Christians.[12]

It is worth noting that one of the places in New York where prayer meetings were held during this period was not a church; it was Burton's Chamber Street Theatre. It was opened for prayer on March 17, 1858, and quickly filled up.

> Half an hour before the time appointed for service, the theatre was packed in every corner from the pit to the roof. By noon the entrances were so thronged that it required great exertions to get within hearing distance, and no amount of elbowing could force an entrance so far as to gain sight of the stage! People clung to every projection along the walls, and they piled themselves upon the seats and crowded the stage beneath, above and behind the curtain. The street in front was crowded with vehicles, and the excitement was tremendous. Nearly all the assembly were businessmen, only two hundred being ladies and fifty clergymen.[13]

By the time the revival spread through New York City, not only were the Methodists and the Dutch Reformed churches involved, but the Episcopal, Union, Congregational, YMCA, Presbyterian, and Baptist constituencies were all praying with packed churches and beginning to see some startling conversions. In fact, "A Baptist journal attempted to keep abreast of the news of conversions reaching its offices, but the editor apparently gave up the task after listing seventeen thousand conversions reported to him by the Baptist leaders in three weeks."[14]

Now the secular media was beginning to take notice, and for good reason. Humanity appeared to be connecting with God. Evidence shows that lives and nations were being changed because of it. According to Orr:

> By March of 1858, the secular press was giving lengthy columns to the intelligence of the awakening . . . Why did the editors of the various papers give such space to a religious movement?

---

12. Please note that the *Christian Advocate* from New York names a John Street Church in the revival in New York, which is not to be confused with the John Street Church in Hamilton, Ontario, Canada.

13. Orr, *Second Evangelical Awakening*, 11.

14. Ibid., 16.

There were three good reasons. Obviously, the awakening was engrossing the whole nation and most people demanded revival news. When a Western editor saw a column generously devoted to religion in a leading New York contemporary, he saw a trend and found the example good. Another reason was found in the startling effects on editors and journalists themselves.[15]

In May of 1858, The *Christian Advocate and Journal*, the New York Methodist newspaper, had an editor collate figures across the United States from as many sources possible. He concluded that a "total of 96,216 people had been reported as converted [to faith in God] in the few months past."[16] Soon, State schools and colleges were affected and the number of converts reached 50,000 a week. The churches added 10,000 converts a week for two years.[17]

When Phoebe was at home in New York City, she kept abreast of the latest news in the spread of the revival, and kept in contact with those in Canada. In an excerpt from one of Phoebe's letters she wrote about the influence of Hamilton abroad.

> A lawyer, who is an earnest class-leader, told me a few hours since, that he took the paper containing the published account of the revival at Hamilton, and read it to the members of his class, instead of engaging in the usual exercise of relating experience. The result was, that the members united themselves into a band to carry out the principles of the letter. The revival in Hamilton is still going on, and at the last advices we were informed that between five and six hundred had been saved.[18]

The awakening was beginning to be characterized as, "The most publicized work of grace [that] was undoubtedly the condition prevailing in the metropolis of New York, but the phenomenon of packed churches and startling conversions was noted everywhere."[19]

---

15. Orr and Roberts, *Event of the Century*, 241.

16. Ibid., 320. Orr gives an original source as an article titled "Revival Messenger" from *The Christian Advocate and Journal*, June 3, 1858, but this reference appears to be wrong.

17. Wilkinson, "Great Awakening Began in Hamilton."

18. Palmer, *Promise of the Father*, 260.

19. Orr, *Second Evangelical Awakening*, 15.

THE BANK COLLAPSE

Some scholars may claim that the American bank collapse of 1857 was the cause of this Great Awakening or revival; I believe there is some open discussion left to be had about this. The Panic of 1857, also known as the Bank Collapse, began in August 24, 1857 when the Ohio Life and Trust Company (with their second main office in New York) began to fail due to fraudulent activities. The Library of Congress's website states the following:

> The major financial catalyst for the panic of 1857 was the August 24, 1857, failure of the New York branch of the Ohio Life Insurance and Trust Company. It was soon reported that the entire capital of the Trust's home office had been embezzled.[20]

If we look at the time lines of the bank collapse closely, we can observe that three weeks later, on September 14, 1857, *The New York Times* began to write that the event had caused suspensions and failures in a few banks across the nation, but considered this only a temporary panic.[21] On October 3, 1857, *Frank Leslie's Illustrated Newspaper* recorded the sinking of the ship *SS Central America*, which was carrying a large amount of the United States reserve of gold and silver. This reserve could not be recovered, adding to the uncertainty of America's financial stability.[22] By October 14, 1857, *The New York Times* indicated that more banks, including New York City banks, were in a financial crisis[23] and the panic was in full force.

An article in *The Christian Advocate* from New York City on March 25, 1858, sheds some light on the way the Panic was being discussed by church leaders and the general public.

> That the Divine providence may prepare the way for the Spirit is certain, but the ways of the Divine hand are beyond our understanding, and cannot be made the basis of a calculation. It is quite probable that the late financial crisis has in some cases been overruled to the spiritual benefit of its victims; but there have been similar revulsions in financial affairs, which were not followed by such consequences. God's ways are not as our ways. He can

20. Today in History, "August 24. The Panic of 1857."
21. "The Financial Panic."
22. Today in History, "August 24. The Panic of 1857."
23. "The Financial Crisis."

make the most trifling event the occasion for the most wonderful changes, because in all cases the efficiency is in himself.[24]

I have no doubt that many people who were affected by the bank failures began to earnestly seek God. It appears that at the start, the awakening in New York was sparked mainly by a move of God that led Christians to fill the churches seeking a spiritual awakening. This then developed into a subsequent move by the believers to pray for God to intervene in the financial situation on behalf of themselves and their country. Prime notes in chapter 4 of his book *The Power of Prayer* that, although no one could point to the financial problems of the times as the cause of the revival, there was a strong call to prayer. In fact he states, "That the commercial distress which followed had its influence to arrest men's minds, and to make them feel their dependence on God, we cannot doubt. But all speculations of this kind will fail to reach the *cause* of this wide-spread work of grace . . ."[25] He notes that the prayer meetings were already in place before the panic.[26] The financial collapse had a small start in the summer and increasingly grew over the fall of 1857. It is interesting to note that on October 14th, as it hit the news fully in New York, Lanphnier's prayer meetings had changed.

In contrast, what was happening in Canada starting on October 8 and 9 was not just among the Christians, but a simultaneous turning of non-Christians to Christ as well. All this, in Canada at least, had nothing to do with the bank collapse that the US was experiencing. The Hamilton Christians took the call of God beyond the doors of the church and into the streets just a few days before the bank collapse became widespread. The first letter that Phoebe Palmer wrote about the revival in Hamilton was written on October 10, 1857, and sent to New York. Although I have not been able to discover when the recipients received the letter, I imagine it was fairly close to the time (due to travel and communications of the era becoming easier and faster) in which *The New York Times* declared the certainty of the bank panic.

We also need to recognize that Phoebe had written a letter on October 14th to her sister stating that 500 people had become Christians in the few short days the Palmers had been in Hamilton. I have not been

24. "The Revival."
25. Prime, *Power of Prayer*, 60–61.
26. Ibid., 61.

able to find documentation of the number of converts on October 14th at the Fulton Prayer Meeting. However, the timelines for both New York and Hamilton simultaneously demonstrate the beginnings of an awakening. The evidence is clear that God was moving in the hearts of men and women within New York and Hamilton around the same time to awaken his people.

Despite whether one would credit events in Hamilton or New York as the beginning of the Second Great Awakening, the evidence is clear that Hamilton was blessed with a revival, and as we are about to discuss in the next section, Christians all over the world who knew about the revival desired a similar move of God. What is most important about this time period is that both the non-Christians and the Christians were beginning to seek God.

UNITED STATES CHURCH LEADERS[27]

As news spread about this wonderful movement of God both in Canada and in the States via telegraph and the trains carrying newspapers, letters, and travelers, church leaders across the United States began to convene (such as the Presbyterians in Pittsburgh, and other conventions in Cincinnati) to discuss the Palmers' success, to determine if this was a genuine movement of God, and how this new life could be brought into their churches. By the first Sunday of 1858, many churches were preaching revival.

The Christian Advocate from New York City on March 25, 1858, began to share the spreading news of the revival, which was now being considered a "great awakening." It is interesting to note in the following paragraphs how the media, the Christians, and the non-Christians responded to the movement of God. For as different as the Creator has made us, there will most likely always be different camps and opinions on all topics.

> Its progress seems like the march of a conqueror, and its presence is like the breath of spring, all-pervading and life-giving. It reaches from the ocean to the Western frontier, and cities, towns and country are alike affected by it; and though it has already continued more than three months, it shows no signs of abatement.

27. The following section depends largely on one primary source: "The Revival," in the *Christian Advocate*. This source is extremely reliable and helpful for understanding the revival.

A striking evidence of the influence of this work is its general recognition beyond merely religious circles. Everybody speaks of the "great awakening" as a well ascertained fact. The secular press, in all parts of the country chronicles its progress as an important item of local intelligence. Newspaper correspondents write of it in their communications, in common with finances, politics, and the weather; and the telegraph is brought into requisition to convey the news of the triumphs of the Gospel from city to city. These things indicate an unusual state of the public mind, and show that it is very widely and powerfully affected. Though less strongly marked in some of its features than former similar visitations, all agree that in extent, and in its hopeful results, the present revival exceeds any with which the American Churches have been favored during the last half century.

The degree of attention devoted to this matter by the secular press, great as it confessedly is, is less remarkable than the tone and spirit in which the subject is treated. Experience has accustomed us to expect from much of the non-religious press of all grades, when the subject is not systematically ignored, either the most apathetic recognition of vital religion, or sneers at the "fanaticism" of its professors, or a kind of patronizing and halfway apologetical confession of some of its incidentally beneficial results. We have been so long used to this state of things that we have learned to expect it as a matter of course, so that this change of tone awakens more lively interest. But the press is only a reflection of the public sentiment, and therefore we may, from its utterances, infer a great and most salutary reaction in the public mind on this subject. Probably the favorable feeling toward the work of religion evinced by the press, may be attributed somewhat to some of the peculiarities of this revival. Generally all strongly marked excitements in matters of religion are offensive to irreligious persons. This is natural. Men are always displeased with exhibitions of emotions with which they cannot sympathize, and especially when they are opposed to their preconceived notions. And as this revival is distinguished for the absence of all strong exhibitions of feeling, whether joyful or otherwise, this cause of offense is taken away; perhaps, too, a more honorable cause may have aided to producing this result.[28]

The article went on to describe both the feeling surrounding the revival and the actions of those involved. This is what made the event unusual for its time.

28. "The Revival."

This absence of excitement is indeed among the most remarkable features of this revival. In all former cases of the kind, among whatever denominations of Christians they may have occurred, strong emotions have attended the progress of religious awakenings. These excitements have indeed presented widely different aspects, according to the various characters of individuals and the different usages of Churches; but generally the power of the spirit of revival has been pretty fairly indicated by the degree of emotion manifested. Not so, however, in this case. That there has been a quickening of the religious feelings of the Churches, and an increase of evangelical efforts, is not to be denied, though it is equally certain that at scarcely any other period has there been less of that kind of religious fervor, which tends to fanaticism. In the midst of the most striking displays of Divine power, there is a wonderful calmness and even coolness among both the actors and subjects of the revival. Christians converse among themselves of the deep things of the Spirit, or with the unconverted of the necessity of conversion, with a quietness such as has not before been witnessed; and persons become awakened, set out to seek religion, and pass through all the stages of repentance and conversion, with a sober self-possession as pleasing as it is unprecedented. For the explanation of this state of facts we have no theory to offer. We are fully persuaded that the whole work is eminently of the agency of the Holy Spirit, and that he orders its operations according to his own sovereign purposes.[29]

The anonymous writer goes on to acknowledge that the church has probably harmed people in its intentions to do well, and thus reaped the attitudes of those hurt. It is always good to understand where criticism comes from.

The sneers and insults which have been cast upon venerable and unassuming ministers of the Gospel, by men in high places, have not been unheeded by an intelligent people, and in the position thus assumed for the Church by her ministers, she commands the public conscience, though she may gain the reproaches of those whose interest she damaged. Never, probably, has the enlightened conscience of the American people more fully sympathized with their ministers than they do at this very time; and the moral power thus given to them, and exerted by them in their

29. Ibid.

ministrations, is now receiving its highest commendations in the magnificent presence and saving power of the Holy Spirit.[30]

Despite the critics, the revival progressed and changed people for the better. The following evidence suggests that secular society was warming up to the church once again. "The progress of this change in the public sentiment, at least in a very considerable portion of society, is well illustrated in the history and the changing attitudes of the *New York Tribune*, in its relations to evangelical Christianity."[31]

The writer finishes off by saying:

> In conclusion, we congratulate our readers and the whole church in view of this gracious visitation of the Spirit. "The Lord has done great things for us, whereof we are glad." It is both our right and our duty to rejoice and give praise. But let us also remember that we are still in the heat of the conflict, and there is yet very much to be done before the powers of sin shall be overthrown, and the reign of Christ becomes universal.

Soon the revival spread past the borders of Canada and the US and leapt across the ocean to affect the rest of the world.

THE WORLD

Evidence indicates that the world took notice as all denominations came together to pray in New York. According to the *Christian Guardian*, "There was no fanaticism, no hysteria, just an incredible movement of the people to pray. The services were not given over to preaching. Instead anyone was free to pray!"[32]

The word about the awakening spread like wildfire catching on dry timber. As a preacher might say, God was moving in a new way, as he usually does when he wants our attention. As Orr put it:

> The influence of the awakening was felt everywhere in the nation. It first moved to the great cities, but it also spread through every town, village, and country hamlet. It swamped schools and colleges. It affected all classes without respect to condition. A Divine influence seemed to pervade the land, and men's hearts were strangely warmed by a Power that was outpoured in unusual

30. Ibid.
31. Ibid.
32. Ibid.

ways. There was no fanaticism. There was remarkable unanimity of approval among religious and secular observers alike, with scarcely a critical voice heard anywhere. It seemed to many that the fruits of Pentecost had been repeated a thousandfold.[33]

What the Christians considered to be a new move of God quickly began to spread from Canada to the United States, Ireland, Jamaica, Scotland, Wales, and England, giving birth to a renewed vision, new movements and churches. Often there were meetings and prayers already in place, but as word of the Spirit's moving came to the world's attention, the movement took hold of more places and people.

"What was extraordinary was its effect, which in years to come made men believe that this thing was of God and not of man," wrote Charles Wilkinson in his article in the *Hamilton Spectator*. "Its most marked feature was that men and women hoped desperately for such a revival as Hamilton had, and then they prayed earnestly for it, and it came."[34]

The following sketches outline what took place as the Second Great Awakening took a hold of places around the world. In order to keep the flow of the storyline, I am documenting the move geographically rather than strictly chronologically.

The Jamaican Revival

By 1860, news of the revival had spread and churches in the colony of Jamaica were praying that revival would capture the Caribbean lands. Workers would gather for early morning prayer before the start of their workday in the plantations, instead of at noon hour. These meetings became known as "peep of the day prayer meetings."[35] By September of that year, a small Moravian chapel in the town of Clifton ignited the flames of revival.

Revival quickly spread across denominational barriers and throughout the Caribbean Islands. Repentance was led mostly by the children attending the meetings, who prayed fervently, which, participants believed, caused the movement to spread rapidly. Many preachers tried to calm the tide of the Spirit's work, often by shutting down

33. Orr, *Second Evangelical Awakening*, 17.

34. Wilkinson, "Great Awakening Began in Hamilton," 18.

35. Orr and Roberts, *Event of the Century*, 207. See also Towns and Porter, *Ten Greatest Revivals Ever*, ch. 5, section on The Jamaican Revival (1860).

the churches after a late service, but failed in their attempts to send the people home. The meeting participants would often relocate and remain in a state of prayer.

Evidence shows that so powerful were the prayers and the movement of the Spirit that many gained a healthy fear of God. Many people had straightened up temporarily, while others could barely believe the power that God extended to them after so much prayer. The people responded to the miraculous work of the Spirit; however, the revival in Jamaica was not as low-key as in America. People reported twitching, and convicted sinners being struck deaf and dumb, or screaming and gnashing of teeth, with clothes torn as the Spirit of God descended.

Throughout the islands, people were drawn to the church and convicted of their sin. In Bethel Town, it was said that "as many as one hundred hardened sinners prostrated at once."[36]

> In a prayer meeting held in one notoriously wicked place, two young women were struck down as though by lightening, where upon one confessed her life of abandon. The two younger men were struck dumb, one of them writhing in agony.[37]

In yet another place, young people were flocking to the church and it was said that, "Backsliders also were seeking pardon and re-admission. Rum shops were less frequented, and the noise made by quarrelsome and tipsy patrons on local roads at night was no longer to be heard."[38]

People were so affected by the moving of the Spirit that they had mixed emotions about it. They embraced both the joy and the fear of God. "While joy possessed the hearts of many, fear fell on the other people. Some believers told their pastor, 'Minister, we have been praying for revival of religion, and now God poured out His Spirit, we all 'fraid for it.'"[39]

People would listen for hours outside the church windows, repent, and begin to live righteously. Couples living together out of wedlock got married. Separated spouses came together again. People sought salvation and church membership. The church had grown so strong and steadily in this part of the world that the London Missionary Society withdrew

36. Orr and Roberts, *Event of the Century*, 207.
37. Ibid.
38. Ibid., 209.
39. Ibid., 207.

and left the work of the gospel to the nationals. In fact, missionaries and money were sent from Jamaica to Africa and the West Indies.[40]

Elmer Towns, in his book *The Event of the Century*, records a report as saying:

> Chapels became once more crowded. There was a widespread conviction of sin. Crime diminished. Ethical standards were raised. There was renewed generosity. Old superstitions, which had reasserted themselves once more, declined in power. As the movement spread, unhealthy excitement and religious hysteria showed themselves in places, but the testimony of almost all observers of whatever denomination was that the Revival did permanent good.[41]

Towns continues with the following, concerning Jamaica:

> The nation of recently liberated slaves had discovered their real liberty in Christ, and most chose not to return to the bondage from which Christ had set them free. Indeed, many also became themselves messengers of the liberating gospel of Christ beyond the shores of the island.[42]

Ulster, Ireland

In September of 1857 James McQuilkin and three other men started a prayer meeting in a schoolhouse near Kells. These men prayed fervently for the unsaved in their community. By December the first fruits of their prayer began to appear. Many count this small meeting as the beginning of the Ulster revival.[43]

Meanwhile, many other prayer meetings were taking place around Ireland, and the country was dreaming of revival. So it was no surprise that by 1859 the Spirit of God began to move in remarkable ways and people came to repent and be saved. Large crowds would gather in churches and the overflow would endure stormy weather in order to hear the preaching that was led by the Spirit.[44]

---

40. Towns and Porter, *Ten Greatest Revivals Ever*, ch. 5, section on The Jamaican Revival (1860).

41. Ibid.

42. Ibid.

43. Towns and Porter, *Ten Greatest Revivals Ever*, 73.

44. Orr, *Second Evangelical Awakening*, ch. 5.

It was reported that due to the revival, "a large distillery, capable of turning out 1,000,000 gallons of whiskey per annum was put up by auction to be sold or dismantled."[45]

In Ulster there was a

> spiritual movement among children and teenagers. It was not uncommon for teenage boys to conduct street meetings among their peers. In these meetings, according to some reports, children would often "swoon, fall down, tremble, shake, and weep." Adults critical of the movement called it "juvenile sickness," but the children responded, "This is not taking ill. It is the soul taking Christ." At one such meeting, an Irish clergyman counted forty children and eighty parents listening to the preaching of twelve-year-old boys.[46]

The children and teens often held meetings and preached in the streets—reaching out to their peers—despite the criticism from their elders. In one incident a schoolboy was sent home with a Christian classmate as he was having a difficult day. On the way home, he fell under conviction and repented. He returned to school, and gave an account of what had happened. His teacher and headmaster were moved. His classmates and other school children could be seen kneeling in prayer in the school yard at recess. The local priests were called in to minister alongside the boy. The child was even asked to comfort and pray for the headmaster.[47]

Edinburgh, Scotland

As the revival flames reached into Scotland, they burned in the hearts of men and women encouraging them to bring the message of Christ to their people. Soon churches were packed. The following is an account of what it was like:

> [Reginald] Radcliffe and [Richard] Weaver, English evangelists, could not get a place large enough for their meetings. On one occasion, 1,800 people crowded the Richmond Place Chapel, whilst thousands more paced the streets outside. Weaver and Radcliffe had to walk on the shoulders of stalwart men in order to alter-

45. Orr, *Second Evangelical Awakening*, 38.

46. Towns and Porter, *Ten Greatest Revivals Ever*, ch. 5, section on The Ulster Revival (1859).

47. Orr, *Second Evangelical Awakening*, 38.

nate ministry inside and outside the chapel. Hundreds remained behind for conversation, even though the preaching had gone on from seven until eleven p.m.[48]

In the end, it was said that "in the first stages of revival there was a seeking to the evangelist, whereas later it became a seeking of the lost by the evangelist."[49] The shift had come. No longer was Scotland looking to the professionals only to evangelize the lost; many had turned and become evangelists themselves.

Cardiff, Wales

Phoebe Palmer visited the Welsh city of Cardiff in 1862 (later it became the capital of Wales). She described the incredible move of God in Cardiff:

> For thirty days a remarkable work of the Spirit was acknowledged and felt throughout the town, affecting public morals and bringing hundreds to the house of prayer, so much so that a town councilor (Anglican) of long experience testified that police cases were dwindling and the detective added that Cardiff had become a different place.[50]

England

In 1859 many of the English had experienced revival under Catherine and Reverend William Booth's ministry during their Methodist circuit chapel travels. One of the chapels, Bethesda Chapel, due to its influence and success with the lost, had earned the name "The Converting Shop."[51]

On January 8, 1860 another ground-breaking occurrence happened.

> It was during these Revival times that Mrs. Catherine Booth (January 8, 1860) announced her intention of preaching—to the astonishment of her husband and congregation. Likewise it was during this Revival that William and Catherine Booth began to preach the doctrine of Full Salvation now an integral part of Salvationist teaching.[52]

48. Orr, *Second Evangelical Awakening*, 47.

49. Ibid., 48.

50. Ibid., 52.

51. Ibid., 57.

52. Ibid.

Catherine and William saw amazing results as they worked together as evangelists. Catherine described some of the people she saw come
to Christ in their meetings:

> One had been a drunken, gambling, prize-fighting hooligan
> who needed five or six policeman to take him to jail. Another
> had been a horse-racer, professional gambler and drunkard. Yet
> another was named "The Birmingham Rough," a wicked and
> abandoned character before his conversion.[53]

Bishop Handley Moule from the English countryside was impacted
by the way people were turning to God in Dorset and in Fordington
England in 1859. He wrote: "For surely it was Divine . . . No powerful
personality, no Moody or Aitken, came to us. A city missionary and
a London Bible-woman were the only helpers from a distance. But a
power not of man brought souls to ask the old question, 'What must I
do to be saved?'"[54]

As the revival went on, and people were drawn to Christ, he wrote
more: "And the church was thronged to overflowing, and so was the spa-
cious schoolroom, night after night throughout the week."[55]

DWIGHT L. MOODY

Dwight L. Moody (a well-known American evangelist and hymn writer)
became a Christian in 1856, just before the revival began.[56] He stated his
belief: "If this world is going to be reached, I am convinced that it must
be done by men and women of average talent."[57]

In 1859 he organized a Sunday School, to which Emma C. Revell,
his future wife, came to help with the teaching.[58] He started his first
Sunday School class by reaching out to the lonely and less fortunate
children in Chicago. Soon the children packed the classroom and larger
quarters were needed, so he moved to a hall in North Market. In just
over a year attendance grew to between 650 and 1,000 children weekly.

---

53. Ibid., 67.
54. Ibid., 63.
55. Ibid.
56. W. R. Moody, *Life of Dwight L. Moody*, 40–42.
57. D. L. Moody, *To the Work*, 87.
58. W. R. Moody, *Life of Dwight L. Moody*, 56.

At that time, he was elected Superintendant of the Mission School.[59] He was an effective evangelist who knew how to reach the hurting hearts of ordinary children and adults, partly due to his personal experience.

Some of Moody's most noted achievements were birthed during the Second Great Awakening, as he spurred on the Sunday School movement, and was instrumental in ministering to the wounded and dying soldiers of the civil war, among other evangelical efforts.[60] Dwight L. Moody's church, which was founded during the revival years, was located in Chicago, Illinois. Long after the revival ended, he continued to participate in doing God's work with tremendous results. In 1871, Moody had taken part of the summer to preach in California; while he was absent, his Chicago flock had scattered.[61]

Upon returning to Chicago, in late summer or early fall, Moody was impressed by the Spirit to preach on the lives of various biblical characters, which drew out the largest crowds he ever encountered. At the end of his series he challenged people with the gospel, asking those in attendance to consider it for a week.[62] That evening a great fire swept the city burning many structures to the ground. The Great Chicago fire burned from Sunday October 8 to Tuesday October 10, 1871. At least 300 people died in that fire, and 100,000 people were left homeless.[63] The weight of the event lay heavily upon Moody so he changed the way he evangelized to encouraging an immediate response to Christ.

Moody was exhausted from the events that had occurred, and in 1872 he traveled to London, England where he was not so well known, to rest and raise money for his church, which had been burned in the fire. Shortly after he arrived, the Reverend Mr. Lessey, a good friend, asked him to share at his Sunday meetings. The first meeting seemed to have very little effect, if any, on those in attendance. Moody was discouraged, but he had promised to preach at the evening service. It is recorded that Moody saw the Spirit of God come in a powerful way, and many people made an immediate commitment to Christ that night. Moody's son recorded the reaction of Moody and Lessey to the event: "The minister was surprised, and so was Mr. Moody. Neither had expected such

59. Chapman, *Life and Work of D. L. Moody*, 92–96.

60. W. R. Moody, *Life of Dwight L. Moody*, chs. 7, 8, 9.

61. Ibid., 144.

62. Ibid., 144–45.

63. Chicago Historical Society, "The Great Chicago Fire."

a blessing. They had not realized that God can save by hundreds and thousands as well as ones and twos."[64]

Moody encouraged the crowd to meet with the local pastor the following evening.

The Rev. Lessey had opened the church the following day to deal with the new believers, but the crowd increased in size. Moody had already left for Dublin, Ireland, so Lessey sent an urgent message, begging Moody to return. Moody recognized God's hand and returned to London to aid in the continuing revival.[65] Moody was used in both America and England to fan the flames of revival.[66]

ELSEWHERE/OTHER MOVEMENTS

In America, the Sunday School movement (which had started in the 1780s) burst into new life with the influence of people such as D. L. Moody and Stephen Paxson, leading and disciplining many toward Christ.[67] The song "Jesus Loves Me" was originally a poem penned in 1858 by Anna Bartlett Warner of New York, put into the mouth of a character in a book that her sister co-wrote. The character used it to reach out and comfort a dying child. A few years later William Batchelder Bradbury put the poem into song and added the chorus. The following is Anna Bartlett's original poem:

> Jesus loves me—this I know,
> For the Bible tells me so;
> Little ones to him belong,—
> They are weak, but he is strong.
>
> Jesus loves me—loves me still,
> Though I'm very weak and ill;
> From his shining throne on high,
> Comes to watch me where I lie.

---

64. W. R. Moody, *Life of Dwight L. Moody*, 153.

65. Ibid. Some people see this as still part of the Great Awakening, while others see a new movement here. Also the thoughts of Mr. Moody in regards to the new way he saw God move in this time are quite enlightening to the person desiring to study revival. I believe that God is creative and full of surprises.

66. Towns and Porter, *Ten Greatest Revivals Ever*, ch. 5, section on Moody's British Campaign (1872).

67. Ibid., ch. 5, section on Sunday School Revival.

Jesus loves me—he will stay,
Close beside me all the way.
Then his little child will take,
Up to heaven for his dear sake.[68]

Many campus and youth ministries were formed during the awakening, sending missionaries to China, India, Japan, and other mission fields, boosting activity in world missions.[69]

As the Civil War broke out in the United States (1860–65), Reverend George Duffield Jr.'s friend, Rev. Dudley A. Tyng, took a stand preaching against slavery. Unfortunately, in March 1858 Tyng lost his life in an accident. George penned and published the hymn for his funeral: "Stand up, Stand up for Jesus." The hymn was used during the Civil War to inspire soldiers.[70]

Women started to become prominent role models in ministry, as a result of the influence of Phoebe and the wave of revival changing both the people and the church's philosophy.[71] The movement also fostered cross-denominational/ecumenical cooperation.[72]

The Salvation Army, formed by Catherine and William Booth in 1865, was inspired by the revival and was initially called "The Christian Mission." Catherine, a close friend of Phoebe, was encouraged to step forward to preach as a female. The YMCA was also formed as a result of this movement.

Albert Benjamin Simpson was converted in the revival in Chatham, Ontario. He started preaching in 1861, and later went to Knox College in Toronto, graduating in 1865. That year, he became the minister of

---

68. "Warner, *Say and Seal II*, 115–16. See also Bradbury, *Golden Trio*, 68, where *Jesus Loves Me* appears in the music. See also Orr and Roberts, *Event of the Century*, 292. Due to the faster and wider spread of communications, many poems turned to hymns and caught on with the general public more quickly than in the past.

69. Towns and Porter, *Ten Greatest Revivals Ever*, ch. 5, section on Campus and Youth Ministries.

70. Challies, "Hymn Stories: Stand Up, Stand Up for Jesus!"

71. See Dayton and Dayton, "Your Daughters Shall Prophesy," 72–78.

72. Phoebe's daughter, Phoebe Knapp, wrote a tune that Fanny Crosby finished and called "Blessed Assurance." The song was later published by Phoebe Palmer in a magazine. This song written by two women is traditionally sung in many denominations today. See Orr and Roberts, *Event of the Century*, 295.

Knox Presbyterian Church in Hamilton, Ontario. He later founded the Christian and Missionary Alliance.[73]

Joseph A. Scriven came from Dublin to Canada in 1845. In 1855, he tragically lost his second wife, and his mother became deathly ill. He penned a poem called "Pray without Ceasing," and some believe it was sent to his mother during her illness.[74] The poem was published and later put to music by Charles Crozat Converse, and given the name "What a Friend We Have in Jesus." It was especially sung throughout the period of the Awakening, to encourage those who were lonely and in despair. Reverend James Cleland eloquently describes the impact of the song in the book *What a Friend We Have in Jesus and Other Hymns by Joseph Scriven*:

> Criminals on the scaffold have requested to have it sung to them. Mr. Van Meter states that it has been sung in the sweet Italian tongue, under the walls of the Vatican. It has sung its way to millions and millions of souls, inspiring comfort and hope in the stormy passages of life.[75]

The largest number of conversions recorded in 1858 were by the Methodists (membership increase of 12 percent), followed by the Baptists (membership increase of 10 percent), then the Presbyterians, Congregationalists, Protestant Episcopalians, Dutch Reformed, and other Presbyterians. It was estimated that over a million people were saved in one year in North America.[76]

Both Orr and Roberts verify that:

> In Ontario, the British related Wesleyan Methodist Conference (not including many Methodist Episcopal congregations of American affiliation) had been gaining 1,700 members a year prior to mid 1857. During 1858, an increase of 7,096 was recorded with 2,646 in 1859, and 1,956 in 1860, still above the 1856–57

---

73. Ibid., 29.

74. Port Hope Scriven Committee, "Joseph Scriven," and Clayton, "Joseph Scriven 1819–1886." I have not been able to confirm proper documentation of the situation that led him to write the poem, but according to these and many websites, it was for his ill mother.

75. Cleland, *What a Friend We Have in Jesus: And Other Hymns by Joseph Scriven*, 6.

76. Orr, *Second Evangelical Awakening*, 70–71.

average. In June 1859, churches reported an enrollment of 51,669 members without counting the adherents and children.[77]

J. Edwin Orr, continues, "The Wesleyans had added about 20 per cent to their 1858 membership through the influx of converts of the Revival Period."[78]

Although there is much more to be discovered about the Revival as it swept many nations and became the Second Great Awakening, I believe that this has been a brief, but good overview of major events. Now the focus of this book will return to Hamilton to explore what happened to the key players, churches, and the surrounding areas.

77. Orr and Roberts, *Event of the Century*, 35.
78. Orr, *Second Evangelical Awakening*, 74.

8

What Happened Next in Hamilton?

A S WITH MANY REVIVALS, people look at what happened from all angles with their own views. Samuel Rice commented on the following events after the revival.

> Discredit has been thrown on the work by some and exaggerated by others. These conflicting rumors seem to demand a statement of facts, and the more so, as some ministers have reported our work here as valueless.
>
> The work itself in power and extent for the time surpasses any work I have seen in the course of my ministry—the efforts put forth differ from any other.[1]

Rev. Rice went on to tell the Methodist newspaper how he organized the new converts into groups so he could help them grow in their Christian journey. He noted that not everyone stayed strong and committed to their faith and journey, which often happens with new converts.

> At the close of three week's labour we undertook the difficult work of forming the classes, and I feel it to be my duty to take a somewhat unusual course relative to the work, believing earnestly as I do in "revivals" and that without them Methodism would be shorn of her strength. I have been attacked on the reaction which frequently follows, and the diminution of numbers resulting. I have always been confident that the falling away has not been so much from the new members. If old members will pass through a season of grace, and not avail themselves of the opportunity to renew their strength, they grieve the Spirit of God, and we have known as a result some terrible back-sliding. Again, there

1. Rice, "The Work of God in Hamilton."

are some leaders and some classes that have a wonderful facility for reducing their numbers, and you need a revival every year to keep such classes from becoming extinct; other classes are full and overflowing. The reason is obvious.

In our recent work we laid it down as a principle not to put the new converts into old classes. Only 80 for fear of convenience sake were put into the previously existing classes. We appointed new leaders, and made up the classes of new converts nearly doubling the number of leaders, so now we fairly test the statement that there is not so great defection in the members brought in by means of revival. So far the plan has succeeded better than we anticipated—the new classes are prosperous—good attendance of members and generally faithful.[2]

SAMUEL RICE

Samuel Rice would help to carry on the work of the revival—for he had seen many in his time. As a leader, he reported how the work progressed in Hamilton, after the Palmers left, in a letter published in the *Christian Guardian*.

The Dr. and Mrs. Palmer remained with us a little over a fortnight after, and in that time and a fortnight after over 600 names were entered on our registry as saved. Some of those had been in the church; some were members—some from the country, and many from other churches in the city, for our meetings were not for proselytism but for salvations, and I doubt not that the registration was in the main a fair index of the results of four week's campaign. This result was reached by the united labours of the membership under the general direction of the above stated. We have had the opportunity of examining the work through two quarterly visitations and by personal pastoral converse. So far as these converts have become connected with us, or have belonged to the families of our people, and we have no hesitancy in saying that if the ordinary evidences that from the beginning have been recognized as valid, are to be relied on, then this work is truly the work of God, bearing His seal indubitably.

Rev. Rice was forthright in saying that some of the converts had been attending church prior to the revival. It would appear by his statements that he still had some questions about the revival, as he spoke

2. Ibid.

with those who entered their names in the registration of salvation. I believe he was recognizing the different factors that could affect people in revival situations such as people potentially being caught up in a large event, or wanting to be a part of a large revival or event and doing what they could to be a part of it. There may also have been people who wanted to meet the celebrities of their day and would do anything to gain their attention. Also, there could have been those who were struggling to understand their own salvation (potentially new and older converts). Rice could also be questioning whether there were other genuine converts that hadn't registered and were being discipled by other believers. However, through two different pastoral visits with each of the new believers (who had registered), Rev. Rice acknowledged that 600 people had committed to becoming Christians. These he believed were solid commitments. He also understood that the new believers needed to keep walking in their faith, lest they backslide. He believed that these 600 proved that the revival was truly the work of God, as they had converted and worked within the church and grew in their faith. This added confirmation to his belief that that the revival was genuine. In fact the three churches increased their membership during this time, making the new count 824 people.[3]

Both Phoebe and Rev. Rice noted that beyond the new conversions others had been justified or received entire sanctification (the filling of the Holy Spirit). This count was different from the new believers, and quite large, showing the even greater impact of the revival.[4]

3. This would mean that more than 324 people joined the church, since he reports that during this time some former members died or left. He implies that some left who did not agree with the revival or with the way the new converts were being handled (Rice, "The Work of God in Hamilton").

4. See ibid., and Phoebe's letter to the *Christian Guardian*, "A Revival after Apostolic Times," in Wheatley, *The Life and Letters of Mrs. Phoebe Palmer*, 332.

Wesleyan Methodist Female (Ladies) College

Later, Rice rose to become head of the Hamilton Methodist Conference, and affected many lives. Eventually he left the pulpit and for fifteen years became the headmaster of Hamilton's first college on King Street between Catherine Street and John Street (near Walnut Street)— Wesleyan Methodist Female College. The college was built in 1861 and was before its time, as it trained women to serve God.[5]

PHOEBE'S THOUGHTS REGARDING THE HAMILTON CONGREGATIONS

As I read through many of Phoebe's letters, it was clear that she often thought of the divine appointment that had occurred in Hamilton. As she traveled in Canada she would try to get back to Hamilton as often as she could. She looked upon the city with fondness. "We were nearly a day passing with the rapidity of steam-power, through Canadian territory. Several large towns lay in our way, over some of which our hearts affectionately lingered, in remembrance of battles fought and victories won for Christ, the Captain of our salvation. Particularly was this the

5. Bailey, *Dictionary of Hamilton Biography*, 170.

case, in passing the towns of London and Hamilton."[6] Phoebe continued to keep Hamilton in her mind and prayers, encouraging the churches to continue the work that God had started.

> *Phoebe's Diary, November 23rd.*—Received a most interesting letter to-day, from Rev. E. B. Harper, Hamilton, C.W. The work is still progressing, though not with the same power as when we left. He says that to just the degree the people continued to work in bringing *one each* day, to just that degree the work prospered; but just as soon as they began to slacken their efforts in this direction, penitents became less numerous, and those that came forward seemed more strengthless in their efforts in coming to the Savior for pardon. What an assurance, that the strength of the church is in the use she makes of proffered grace.
>
> Just so soon as the church in Hamilton began to labor, and travail for souls, just so soon, and proportionately speedy, were souls born into the kingdom of Christ. And proportionately strong were these children born to the church.
>
> I wrote a farewell letter, which was read at the quarterly love feast. In this letter, I urged the necessity of continuous work, and assured them, if the work should cease, that the responsibility might be on the membership. The next day the membership went newly to work, and the altar was again well-nigh surrounded with penitents.[7]

THE CHURCHES TODAY

The original Hamilton church buildings involved with the 1857 Hamilton Revival no longer exist. The churches either burned to the ground, or required replacing, as most were made of wood or other material that decays over time. The creation of the United Church of Canada in 1925 merged virtually all of the Methodist churches, two-thirds of the Presbyterian churches, some pre-existing union churches and the Congregational churches in Canada under one umbrella. It made sense to do this, according to Semple.

> The central feature of Methodism's crusade for spiritual and moral progress during the twentieth century was ecumenical cooperation and the union of Protestant forces into one dy-

---

6. Wheatley, *The Life and Letters of Mrs. Phoebe Palmer*, 418. This letter is from 1857.

7. Ibid., 333.

namic national church. It did not advocate its own demise, but rather believed that its great commission to spread Christianity throughout the world could be best fulfilled within a broadly Protestant institutional framework. The Canadian Methodist church concluded that there remained little or no justification for a divided Canadian Protestantism while a world of opportunity awaited untied action. It seemed improbable that Christ's earthly rule could arrive as long as Christians continued in their narrow, competing denominations. All Christians throughout the world belonged to the same family, shared the same values, and worked for a common end. Under God's benevolent direction, this family must eventually harness its efforts into one collective whole in order to meet the challenges of evil.[8]

According to Semple, it was an effective amalgamation. "In establishing a polity for the United Church of Canada, the Basis of Union suggested that the corresponding levels of courts in the three churches, despite differences in names, carried on essentially the same functions and that where they differed, they could still contribute to the overall welfare of the denomination. The local congregations could therefore retain familiar structures if they wished, and the United Church would amalgamate names, practices, and structures."[9] He goes on to say that, "Over time, as theological and doctrinal differences had declined in importance, the Presbyterians, Congregationalists, and Methodists had come to share a common ethos, with similar views on the sacraments, the nature and function of ministry, and common approaches to secularism and modernism. As well, they were most self-consciously Canadian of the churches and shared a common desire to assimilate native peoples and new immigrants and a similar dynamic national vision."[10]

All of the Hamilton Methodist churches became part of the United Church of Canada. They believed this would help to spread the good news, create God's kingdom on earth, and promote building up Canada as a Christian nation by providing a church for the nation.[11]

8. Semple, *The Lord's Dominion*, 416.

9. Ibid., 422.

10. Ibid., 424.

11. Ibid., 424, 427, 439.

The King Street Church

First Place, where First Methodist Church once stood.

First-Pilgrim United Church]

The King Street Wesleyan Methodist Church building would eventually be replaced several times; the last two times fire destroyed everything. The King Street Church was renamed First Methodist in 1875. First

Methodist became a part of the United Church of Canada in 1925, and was then renamed First United Church.

In 1963, Central United Church (formerly Central Methodist) amalgamated with First United Church (formerly First Methodist Church).[12] When the last fire destroyed the First United Church in 1969, it was decided that First Place, affordable apartments for the elderly and those with special needs, would be built on this sacred ground.[13]

The First United Church congregation, in need of a space, held services in the Anglican Church of St. Thomas (at Main Street East and Wellington Street across from First Place) until 1980. In 1980 First United Church moved back into a new home in First Place.[14]

Less than a block away, at 200 Main Street East, was the Pilgrim United Church building (originally it was First Congregational Church until it entered the United Church of Canada in 1925). In 1963, a German Evangelical congregation initiated talks to share a worship space with Pilgrim United.[15] In 1965, the German Church became re-constituted as an independent United Church that met in the Pilgrim Church building. The two congregations shared the space until they amalgamated under the name Pilgrim United Church in 1982.[16] First United then immediately amalgamated with Pilgrim United to become First-Pilgrim United.[17]

First United (formerly Methodist) Church is still honored by First Place in Hamilton; there you can view the gravestones and other aspects of its heritage. First Place was an extension of First-Pilgrim United Church's outreach ministry, until it was taken over in 2007 by the city of Hamilton.[18]

The John Street Church

According to a 1909 article in the Methodist *Christian Herald*, The John Street Church (Wesley Church, also known as "The Brick Church") amalgamated with the Gore Street Church. "It is said that the churches are now only about half filled at the services and that there is accommo-

12. Pawson, *Growing Together*, 20.
13. Ibid., 12, 21, 23, 94.
14. Ibid., 22.
15. Ibid., 43.
16. Ibid., 48.
17. Fayter, interview.
18. Ibid.

dation for both congregations in Wesley Church. The members think it better to have one large, strong congregation than two small churches."[19] The new church changed the name to Central Methodist.[20] Later it would become Central United and merge with First United Church in 1963.[21] An outreach to the elderly and less fortunate had been started by the John Street Church congregation. Despite the congregation moving out of the building in 1955, the old church continued to be used in a similar manner for outreach and recreation under the name of The Wesley Community Centre (Wesley Centre). The new outreach continued under the United Church Hamilton Presbytery, which gave opportunity for other local United Churches to become involved.[22] Permission was granted in 1964 for the outreach to the marginalized in the inner city to be formalized. This outreach would become Wesley Urban Ministries.[23] As for the John Street church building, the structure was demolished after 97 years in 1975.[24]

The MacNab Street Church

As the revival progressed the need for space in the Hamilton churches became apparent.

The King Street Wesleyan Church's building (First Methodist Church) was now old. Plans for a larger church building were in the works. The building of John Street Church could no longer be added to. It already housed five to six thousand people. This was one of the reasons why the MacNab Street church had continued to be used during the time of the Revival; now it as well was too small. Despite the plans for the King Street Church construction, more space was still needed.

It was decided that the MacNab Street church would eventually be dismantled and the stones and beams from this church were moved piece by piece up to King and Wellington Streets to build a new King Street Wesleyan Church (later to be known as First Methodist Church). This was done according to the Methodist philosophy of "waste not, want

19. "Fine Record of Wesley," 11.
20. Ibid., 12. See also Wesley United Church (Hamilton, Ont.) fonds.
21. Pawson, *Growing Together*, 20.
22. Baldwin, "City's Wesley United Church Counts History back to '78."
23. Wesley Urban Ministries, "Our History."
24. "The Wrecking Crew."

not." The MacNab Street church was located on the corner of MacNab Street and Merrick Street, which no longer exists because the construction of York Boulevard took over that intersection. The church was long gone before plans for the Hamilton Market, the Mall, and Copps Coliseum (now FirstOntario Centre) ever existed. This is my best guess at where the old site was located.

True to the resourceful nature of the Methodists, the MacNab Street church was demolished and the stones and beams were reused in the new building or the replacement of the King Street church. People coined the name "New Stone Church" for the new church replacing King Street church. In the book *Growing Together: A History of First-Pilgrim United Church, Hamilton, Ontario*, the church demolition is noted in the following way: "The old Stone Church was dismantled, each stone and each piece of timber being carefully marked. Piece by piece it was conveyed to the King Street Church Site and rebuilt."[25] The *Hamilton Spectator* also documented the Methodists' resourcefulness in the Thursday February 16, 1869 paper, the day of dedication for the "New Stone" church: "The new edifice, the one to be formally opened and dedicated to-day [The King Street church], is built almost entirely of material from the old McNab [sic] street church, of which it may be considered a sort of second edition, enlarged, ornamented and improved." It continues on to say, "The organ, also from the old Mc Nab [sic] street church . . . is not yet entirely rebuilt."[26]

---

25. Pawson, *Growing Together*, 9. See also Sutherland, *1869 City of Hamilton Directory*, 50.

26. "Dedication."

Centenary (Methodist/United) Church Outside (circa 1900)

Centenary (Methodist/United) Church Inside

A new church called Centenary Methodist (later, Centenary United) would be built in 1866–68, and it would house the overflow of people that the original churches could not contain (as each church's seating only allowed for five to six thousand). The MacNab Street congregation amalgamated with Centenary, probably due to its proximity and because Centenary was the newest church.[27] The name Centenary was given to the church because it celebrated the 100th anniversary of the first known Methodist meeting house in North America. The first Methodist meeting house, built in 1766, was located on Williams Street in New York. It was called the Wesley Chapel.[28]

SURROUNDING AREAS

The Methodist Campground "Grimsby Park"

As the revival continued, the gospel continued to flourish in the areas surrounding Hamilton. In Hamilton's backyard, a Methodist campground was founded in 1860, in Grimsby, Ontario. People from Toronto, the rest of Ontario, and the Northeastern United States for years would flood the grounds to hear the word and the preaching of the circuit ministers.[29] In fact, around September of 1865, Phoebe Palmer arrived by steamer and preached at the Grimsby campground, stating that it was a blessed time. According to her letter dated August 31, 1865, the Palmers were able to return for a service in Hamilton, because they were close by.

27. *The Centenary Story*. Centenary United recently amalgamated with St. Giles United Church and is called New Vision United Church.

28. Ibid.

29. Turcotte and Jarvis, *Greetings from Grimsby Park*.

There she "surveyed the battle ground, where about five hundred were saved in eighteen days."[30]

Many say that because the campground was built after the spiritual interest of the awakening had waned, its lifespan was short. Later it was sold and became an amusement park. Many of the cottages built for the camp meeting, affectionately known as "gingerbread cottages," can still be seen today at the old site.[31]

It had been an amazing four or five months in the life of the Wesleyan Methodist Church. As Orr put it, "The Wesleyans added about 20 per cent to their 1858 membership through the influx of converts of the Revival period."[32]

30. Wheatley, *Life and Letters of Mrs. Phoebe Palmer*, 411.
31. Turcotte and Jarvis, *Greetings from Grimsby Park*.
32. Orr, *Second Evangelical Awakening*, 74.

9

Conclusion

IT ALL STARTED IN Hamilton, out of one prayer meeting in which the participants believed that God moved in their hearts to start something big. Unbeknownst to them at the time, their actions would be used as inspiration around the world during the Second Great Awakening. Participants believed that despite the difficulties Hamiltonians had faced that year, God was still interacting with their lives, and the city was important to God. The evidence suggests that the revival offered reassurance and encouragement to those involved, and they believed that God was still sovereign, and was offering hope and new life to those who were in need. Even though 1857 started poorly it would end on an entirely different note, as a result of those involved listening to what they believed God was directing them to do.

I think that perhaps Hamilton had experienced so many disappointments that God chose to use the Christians living there to make a significant mark on the world by helping to start the Second Great Awakening.[1] This would not be surprising, considering how we see God acting in the events recorded in the Bible. God has often done things differently than what human wisdom might have chosen. For example, he used Moses, a fugitive who stuttered, to help Israel to escape from Egypt (see Exodus). He chose David, the last and smallest child, as a king for Israel from a family of what appeared to be more worthy men (1 Samuel 16:1–13). He sent to Israel as their Savior Jesus, who was born in a stable

---

1. As discussed above, what happened in Hamilton, Canada, was distinct, but can be linked to what was unfolding in New York. I cannot help but conclude that the Hamilton Revival was just as significant, with its timelines and importance to the beginning of the awakening movement, as what happened in New York.

from a descendant who lived in one of the smallest towns in the country, leaving many to question how God's Messiah could possibly come from the backwoods region of Galilee (Matthew 1; Luke 1–2; John 1:46; 7:52).

Although some scholars may pass Hamilton over when they count the places where the Second Great Awakening began, perhaps because of its low status and rough reputation, or even because of a desire to credit New York for being the place where the revival began, the evidence offered in this work suggests the possibility that the Hamilton Revival was really part of the Awakening's beginnings. Personally, I believe that the evidence is clear that God used Hamilton (a backwoods town compared to the metropolises of the United States, the United Kingdom, and Europe) to become an example for Christians as to how they might choose to spread the gospel to those facing issues akin to financial insecurity, debates over the introduction of Darwinism, slavery, and the American Civil War, among other challenges and hardships.

Certainly it is evident in the writings of Phoebe Palmer that events in Hamilton had an impact on many with whom she came in contact. She recorded a few examples of those who had read her widely-published newspaper articles, or heard her speak of what happened in Hamilton in 1857, and were inspired to action because of it. I believe that there were many more of these examples both locally (such as Mrs. Boice's obituary that states the impact of the revival on herself) and around the world that have yet to be found.

I encourage readers to understand and reflect on Phoebe Palmer's simple philosophy. It demonstrates what happens when people follow what they believe to be the principles of the Bible and the voice of God: "Just as justification occurs when the individual turns to the Lord in repentance and faith, so revival occurs when those who profess to be Christians turn to the Lord and begin to serve Him aright."[2] Therefore, Phoebe states that revival can start anywhere, even in a town (or a city) that struggled like Hamilton, if the hearts of those involved are right with God.

A godly woman named Gillian Owensby, in a sermon preached in a small church in Hamilton in 2013, said, "No revival ever started without a prayer meeting."[3] I agree, but there is also the importance of prayer mixed with fearless evangelism. Phoebe encouraged Christians to make

2. White, *Beauty of Holiness*, 166.

3. Owensby, Sermon.

evangelism easy, and not something to be feared. In an 1854 letter, she wrote about the simplicity of blessing and saving others. Those truths still stand today:

> The duty of acting on the principle of entire consecration was at once suggested. Yet, I had not the witness of holiness. But said the Spirit, "Go to work for God—Invite the sinners to Christ." My trembling heart replied . . . "How little do I know of the deep things of God. How little grace have I received; and with such a small amount, how can I dispense to the spiritual necessities of others?" "You can dispense according to what you have received. If you cannot talk about the deep things of God, and explain the mysteries of the kingdom, you can deal in the first principles of the doctrine of Christ. You know men are sinners, and need salvation. You know that they need the invitations of the Spirit to come to Christ. You know they must repent or perish. You know these things because you have read your Bible. Many who profess to believe the Bible, seldom read it. You can go to those who need to be told of the first principles of a religious life, and be a channel of communication from God. Let the Bible speak through you. Sinners will be responsible for these messages of salvation, not because *you* have spoken, but they will be responsible to God, for it is the *Lord's* message, *not yours* that you deliver."[4]

As Charles Wilkinson, former religious editor for the *Hamilton Spectator*, in his 1981 article titled "Great Awakening Began in Hamilton" says, "Could the time be ripe for such another Awakening, I asked in my earlier article. And that it might start in much the same way, with a few people—just a few people who believe that with God all things are possible—praying in Hamilton? Who knows? Who can possibly tell? More things are wrought by prayer than this world dreams of."[5]

For those of Christian faith, I echo his sentiment for today, and encourage us not just to pray, but to put our faith into action. Remember: God is always doing something new. He only parted the Red Sea once (Exodus 13–14); he allowed Jesus to be nailed to the cross once and for all (Matthew 27, Mark 15, Luke 23, John 19), and he sent the tongues of fire to settle above the disciples' heads at Pentecost once (Acts 2). I encourage Christians to read the signs of the times in whatever part of the world they live, to look for what God is doing right now, and seek to be a

---

4. Wheatley, *Life and Letters of Mrs. Phoebe Palmer*, 201.

5. Wilkinson, "Great Awakening Began in Hamilton."

part of that, and then get on board with it. I urge us, in accountable communion with other Christians, to be careful to listen to him and do only what he tells us to. There is no single blueprint for revivals. There are many ways of serving God faithfully. Phoebe did what she believed God had called her to do. The Christians responded to that belief and witness. The results were considered truly remarkable by those involved. I have told Hamilton's story about a revival that took place in 1857. Hamilton's history does not mean this is to be, or should necessarily be, replicated by others everywhere, nor should we get caught up in copying others. It was special for that time and place. We are wise to acknowledge the past, but when we listen to God's direction for ourselves and our churches today, God can assist us in spreading his good news. The principles of praying, listening, and being obedient are what we can copy from any revival. I believe that some of the greatest revivals and movements of God began with these principles. It didn't matter who the Christians were, or where they were from. It was as simple as listening and doing. I believe that if our hearts are open, God will come again in a powerful way; after all it is his nature to desire relationship and restored communication with us.

Appendix

Revival Letters and Documents

NOTE: ALL LETTERS AND documents are transcribed as accurately as possible from the earliest published versions with no additions or changes. I have ordered them according to event timelines. When C.W. appears in letters, it stands for Canada West (= Ontario). All italics, sentence structure, spelling, punctuation and typographical errors are reproduced as they are in the earliest published versions.

Mr. Richard Wheatley, who wrote Phoebe's life and collected her letters, knew the Palmers personally, and traveled with them as a preacher. His book was published by W. C. Palmer, likely the Palmers' son. Mrs. S. A. Lankford was Phoebe's sister (older by one year), Sarah Worrall, who married Thomas Lankford and lived in the same house with Phoebe and Walter. Mrs. Melinda Hamline was Phoebe's life-long friend, who married Bishop Leonidas L. Hamline.

EXTRACTS FROM RICHARD WHEATLEY, THE LIFE AND LETTERS OF MRS. PHOEBE PALMER

This book was first published in New York City by W. C. Palmer Jr., in 1876, and the extract below is from pages 328–34.

HAMILTON, *October 10th*, 1857.

To MRS. S. A. LANKFORD:

We arrived at Hamilton about dark, and Dr. P. made an effort to check his baggage through for Friday, so as to reach home by the Albany boat on Saturday morning. But God has, in a wonderful manner, detained us at every step. Dr. P. was frustrated in his attempt to leave his baggage, and we went to the house of a friend, to remain over night, intending to leave for home early in the morning. It was the usual evening for prayer-meeting in the three churches here. Two of the ministers received information of our unexpected visit, and before we had finished our tea, were with us. They immediately made arrangements for uniting the prayer-meetings. As we proceeded to the meeting, the Spirit of the Lord urged the test, "Call upon me and I will answer thee, and show thee great and mighty things, things that thou knewest not." And while talking in the meeting, I felt a Divine power pressing me mightily to urge upon the people to set themselves apart at once, to work for God in promoting a revival. I felt the Holy Spirit working in my own heart powerfully, and assured the people if they would at once "bring all the tithes into the Lord's store house," and prove Him therewith, that He would open the windows of heaven and pour out such a blessing as would overflow the regions round about, and result in hundreds on hundreds being brought home to God. I asked that as many as would thus bring all the *tithes of time, talent, estate etc.*, into the Lord's treasury, and begin *at once* to act on the principle that the tithes of *time, reputation, talents*, whether of influence, estate, body or mind, should be devoted to the work of soul saving, would manifest their resolve to do so by raising the right hand. Thirty, perhaps, or more of those present lifted their hand in the solemn presence of God that they would begin to work *immediately*. Thus it was that the battle was at once, in the most unlooked-for manner, pushed to the gate. One of the ministers, speaking of this since, said, "The battle was set in array so suddenly, that Satan himself had not time to contemplate a defence." We *dared* not leave, but promised in case that all would thus go abroad at once, and give the gospel invitation, we would remain with them over the next evening. There were in all, probably about sixty or seventy present at the meeting. During the night, my spirit was awake with God, much of the time, and I received a divine conviction that God was about to bring out the people in multitudes and stamp our ideas of a "laity for the times," with signal success. The minister stationed here felt in the same way, on all sides it was agreed that the body of the large and most central church had better be opened. Hundreds came out, though it was not the usual meeting night, and nothing was known of the meeting, only as the gospel invitations had spread rapidly from one to another, to come out and seek salvation. The invitation for seekers of salvation to come to the altar, had not been given more than five minutes, I think before the altar was crowded. Before the meeting closed, twenty-one earnest seeking penitents were rejoicing in God. The most, or all of these, were persons gathered in from the world, and brought to the house of God, the evening previous. You will not wonder that we dared not leave now. The next day, which was Saturday, we had a meeting in the afternoon for the church, and in the evening again for the sinners, when the number out was still more surprising, and over twenty were saved. Yesterday (Sabbath,) we had about thirty saved during the day—in all, about seventy-five in three days. Surely these are the Lord's doing, and marvelous in our eyes. We intend to return home just so soon as the work seems fairly established, so that we dare to leave [pp. 328–30].

HAMILTON, C.W. *October 14th, 1857*

To Mrs. S. A. LANKFORD:

Could we tell you of what we are daily witnessing of God's wonder-working power, in sanctifying believers, and saving sinners, you would be assured that your disappointment is God's appointment. One week ago to-day, such a work commenced in Hamilton, as has never been witnessed before. Between one and two hundred have been translated out of the kingdom of darkness into the kingdom of God's dear Son. Last night, forty-five were saved; the evening previous, thirty, and the evenings previous, about twenty each evening.

Such a Sabbath as yesterday, we never saw. Meetings were being held from seven o'clock in the morning till ten in the evening, in all of which I believe some were saved. We have had but very little preaching. I mean preaching in the technical sense, according to the idea of preaching in the present day. And though I would not be understood to speak lightly of the value of well beaten oil for the service of the sanctuary, yet never have I been so confirmed in a belief long since adopted, in regard to the sort of preaching in the present day. It is the preaching of apostolic times, when all the church membership were "scattered throughout the regions of Judea and Samaria, *except* the apostles." And these scattered bands, of newly baptized disciples, though so young in the faith, and composed of men, women, and children, went everywhere preaching the Word. Surely, dear Sister Sarah, this, in the most empathetic sense, is the sort of preaching which has been made instrumental in this great revival. Though few churches can boast of such ministers for talent and devotedness, and we are earnest in our acknowledgements that as shepherds of this newly gathered flock, their care and also affectionate teachings and guidance, are *absolutely* needful, yet we again say, that though favored with the constant aid of their three resident ministers, and other ministers, visitors of high position, district chairmen, etc.—yet this revival took its rise mainly with the laity. It did not commence in laborious pulpit effort, neither has it progressed in this way. We had but one very short sermon, during the whole week. One of the ministers would generally say a few introductory stirring words, and then leave the meeting with ourselves, to follow up the remarks. Dr. P.'s prayer-meeting tact is of course brought into constant requisition, to bring up the rear.

The result was, that on Sunday, *over one hundred* received the blessing of pardon, before the close of that eventful meeting. Was not this one of the days of the Son of Man? Truly did our hearts say, "This is the day that the Lord hath made, we will rejoice and be glad in it." It is with exceeding carefulness that we speak of these wonderful displays of saving power. The revival has been progressing ten days, and nearly four hundred souls have been newly gathered into the fold of Christ. In the meantime the great work of purification in the church has been going on with great power. Our afternoon meetings are mostly on this subject, and are very largely attended. We commenced them in the lecture room, but were soon crowded out, and compelled to resort to the body of the large church. And it is seldom we have a meeting, but many new witnesses are raised up to testify of the power of Christ to save the uttermost. There has been no attempt to take the number of the wholly sanctified, but from our personal observations, we know that many have received the baptism of the Holy Ghost.

If you think the contents of this letter would interest the attendants on the Tuesday meeting, you are at liberty either to read it, or to relate such portions of it as you think will redound to the *glory of God*. That thus through the thanksgivings of many, *praises* many redound to God.

P.S.—Dr. P—just tells me that five hundred have been saved. Alleluia, the Lord God omnipotent reigneth! [pp. 330–32].

Summarizing the results of the summer and fall campaign, in a letter to Bishop and Mrs. Hamline, on November 13th, Mrs. Palmer says:[1]

Never have we witnessed such triumphs of the cross as during the past summer and fall. I think I should speak more than within bounds, were I to tell you that not less than two thousand have been gathered into the fold, at various meetings we have

1. This would have been November 1857, as are the following two excerpts.

attended. Hundreds of believers have been sanctified wholly, and hundreds have received baptisms of the Holy Ghost, beyond any former experience. We feel that we are also ourselves getting nearer to the heart of Christ, and that all the sympathies of our being, are flowing out in unison with the world's Redeemer.

We went from Hamilton to London, because we dared not do otherwise. The London friends having *claims* on us in a way which I cannot now take time to state. We thought we could not remain, as Dr. P's business seemed so peremptorily calling him home. But the Lord soon began to work in London, much as in Hamilton, and when we tore ourselves away from London, at midnight, after remaining twelve days, the number of the newly saved amounted to about two hundred. We left amid a scene of power, and we trust that the work is still going on, but of this we have not had time to hear, since our return. I need not add the work of entire sanctification has also been going on gloriously, at all of their meetings. Hundreds have received the baptism of the Holy Ghost. Never have we had so much occasion to feel that we are immortal till our work is done.

Diary, November 23rd.—Received a most interesting letter to-day, from Rev. E. B. Harper, Hamilton, C.W. The work is still progressing, though not with the same power as when we left. He says that to just the degree the people continued to work in bringing *one each* day, to just that degree the work prospered; but just as soon as they began to slacken their efforts in this direction, penitents became less numerous, and those that came forward seemed more strengthless in their efforts in coming to the Saviour for pardon. What an assurance, that the strength of the church is in the use she makes of proffered grace.

Just so soon as the church in Hamilton began to labor, and travail for souls, just so soon, and proportionately speedy, were souls born into the kingdom of Christ. And proportionately strong were these children born to the church.

I wrote a farewell letter, which was read at the quarterly love feast. In this letter, I urged the necessity of continuous work, and assured them, if the work should cease, that the responsibility might be on the membership. The next day the membership went newly to work, and the altar was again well-nigh surrounded with penitents.

Of subsequent labors in New York, and its vicinity, no special re-cord seems to have been preserved. That they were abundant indeed, the following excerpt from a letter to Bishop and Mrs. Hamline, on the 5th of December will show:

> We have been called to attend several special meetings in and about New York, at Willimasburg, Perth Amboy, Bedford, Brooklyn etc. We have also received an official letter of invitation from British North America, taking in Nova Scotia, New Brunswick, Prince Edward's Island, Newfoundland, Bermuda, etc. and the friends are also expecting us in Europe. (pp. 332–34)

EXCERPTS FROM THE CHRISTIAN GUARDIAN

The following is taken from the front page of *The Christian Guardian* 29 no. 9, Wednesday, December 2, 1857. The article is titled "A Revival after Apostolic Times." *The Christian Guardian* was published in Toronto.

Hamilton, C.W., October 26th, 1857

MY BELOVED SISTER T.—How little did I think, when parting with you on the Oakville camp-ground, that we should have lingered in those regions till this time. We paused here on the evening of the day we left you with the expectation of tarrying but for the night. But the Angel of the Covenant in the infinitude of His love and wisdom has withstood us in our homeward progress thus far.

On the evening of the day we came here, from fifty to seventy-five of the brethren and sisters assembled as usual, on Thursday evening, for the weekly prayer meeting. About thirty or forty of those were induced to signify their resolve to bring all the tithes into the Lord's store-house, and prove him herewith, and see if he would not pour out a blessing that there should not be room to receive it, so that its overflowings might reach not only this community, but all the regions round about.

RIGHT HAND PLEDGE

I cannot say how many, but from thirty to forty I should judge, solemnly raised their right hand, in affirmation that they were resolved on coming up to the help of the Lord at once. We promised that we would delay for one day our anticipated return home, if each one would resolve on bringing one with them the ensuing evening. This resolve was more than kept by both ministers and members. The basement of the church was found wholly insufficient to contain the people that came out of the ensuing evening, and the body of the church was resorted to. Meetings were appointed for the next afternoon and evening. Ever since meetings, which have been very largely attended, have been held both day and evening. At first the afternoon meetings were held in the basement of the church, but this was soon found to be wholly insufficient, and both afternoon and evening meetings have been held in the body of the church, and have been gloriously owned of God in this awakening and conversion of sinners, and in the entire sanctification of believers, and the general upbuilding of the church.

A GREAT FEATURE OF THE REVIVAL

The efforts of the Ministers here, as Pastors of the flock over which the Holy Ghost hath made them overseers, are beyond praise, but their record is on high; and the Great Shepherd of the sheep will reward them. But the great feature of this revival is the activity of the membership. Not only does the Spirit say come!—but the *Bride*, in her individual membership is saying *come!* And him that heareth is also saying *come!* Hundreds are flocking to the house of God, scores on scores of whom are brought by personal, earnest entreaty; many of whom have been habitual neglectors of salvation, and also of the means of grace.

This revival is, by the blessing of God, the result of a *"Laity for the Times."* A *Ministry for the Times* is all-important, but it does not take the place of a *Laity for the Times.* Our good Ministers here speak of it as a MODEL REVIVAL, and never have we witnessed a revival that might so worthily be enstamped with this appellation.

CONVERTS AND SEEKERS PLEDGE TO WORK

Every evening does the membership, in connection with those *newly* saved, pledge themselves anew with uplifted hand before God and his people, to work in a new subject under the dominion of Christ: and thus the young converts and even seekers, are being trained to work for God. Yes, even he that heareth is also saying *come!* And is not this laying the foundation for a model church. What desirable trainings for young converts! Surely this may in many regards be termed a model revival. By referring to Acts, 8th chap., you will perceive that it is a revival after the foundation of *Apostolic times,* when men and women of the laity went everywhere preaching the word,—that is proclaiming glad tidings—good news—going into the highways and hedges and *compelling people to come in.*

"ALL AT IT AND ALWAYS AT IT"

It is also a revival after the fashion of *primitive Wesleyan Times*. "They are all at it and always at it." So said an eminent Divine, as characteristic of the early Methodists. Methodism might indeed be distinguished as "Christianity in earnest," if such a revival might become general in Europe and America. Everywhere, where Methodists of this sort might plant themselves might it be said, "These men which turn the world upside down, have come hither also."

And in other respects, beyond what I have room to state, is this a model revival. The church is apprehending the importance of conformity to *Scripture!* And *Wesleyan* views in regard to the use of every diversity of talent. The necessity of bringing all the tithes into the Lord's store-house is being recognized.

SANCTIFICATION IN ITS EARNEST SIGNIFICANCE IS RECOGNIZED

The doctrine of *Entire Sanctification* is being apprehended in its earnest significance. We have never believed in a profession of entire sanctification consistent with conformity to the world. It implies as every intelligent Bible reader will readily discern, separation:—Separation from the spirit and practice of the world. Come out from among them and be ye separate, is the Divine command. "Be not conformed to the world." Whose adorning let it not be "of gold or pearls or costly array." Old professors and young converts are putting aside their outward adornings, and in manifestation giving evidence of their belief that Entire Sanctification implies *separation from the spirit of the world.*

I will pause a moment longer here to say, that I think there is a danger of setting the doctrine of entire sanctification too low. It is possible that some earnest seekers may be hindered from attaining the grace by setting it too high, or more properly for want of *simplified views* of the state. But it has ever been a source of regret with me, that persons should imagine that they had attained to a state of entire holiness and were living in the enjoyment of it, the manifestations of whose life evince that they have not received the full baptism of the Holy Ghost.

ENTIRE SANCTIFICATION AND THE BAPTISIM OF FIRE IDENTICAL

Abraham did not go away and leave his sacrifice until after it had been consumed. The baptism of fire stands in close and inseparable connection with the blessing of entire sanctification implying the evident absorption of the entire being in the service

of Christ. And if evident manifestations of love to the world prevail, and the powers of mind, body, and estate are not so devoted
as to give evidence of an absorption of interest in the Redeemer's
kingdom, then such evidences of entire sanctification as the
world has a right to demand are wanting. Holiness and a con-
suming zeal for the general upbuilding of Zion are concomitant
blessings, standing in absolute connection. And what does the
reception of the blessing of holiness imply, but the reception of
the full baptism of the Holy Ghost, as we received on the day of
Pentecost.

CONCLUSION

And now in conclusion what shall I say of the wonders of
grace which God hath wrought. We paused at this place with the
expectation of remaining but a few hours; but hours have multiplied into days until the eighteenth day since our arrival is now
being numbered. Would that I could permit my pen to pause and
recite the signal displays of grace we have seen. Seldom has a
day passed but we have witnessed at least twenty newly born into
the kingdom of Christ, till now the recipients of grace number
at least four or five hundred. The Secretary of the meeting informed me last night that the number of those wholly sanctified
was about two hundred; but both classes not a few are from surrounding country, and the above estimate is probably below the
actual number, as many names, especially of those who received
entire sanctification, were not recorded. I saw a man and his wife
to-day who had come seventy-five miles expressly in view of
coming to the meeting, and sharing in the shower of grace now
falling. They came hungering and thirsting after righteousness,
and returned this morning to their home, filled with the joys of
a full salvation, to spread, we trust the holy flame in their own
region. Three or four Ministers also, from the surrounding stations have received the witness of Holiness, whose faith, we trust
many of their people may be induced to follow. Instances of exceeding interest come crowding upon my mind, the narration of
which would, I am sure call forth the burst of praise from your
ever attuned lips: but here my pen must pause; opportunity fails.
We must leave for London to-day, having given the friends some
encouragement to expect us, in answer to an earnest invitation to
spend a short time with them.

If my time will admit, I may write you of the progress of the
work of London. Of our Toronto friends we have many dear
names written indelibly on our heart. Especially do we remember
the Friday evening prayer circle, of whom our dear Dr. and Mrs.

Robinson and Rogers &c. form a part. We beg you will remember
us to all these, and ask in our behalf, their continual interces-
sion. We also remember with much interest, your dear Ministers,
Borland Douglass &c., and pray that the most enlarged desire of
their hearts may be answered in extraordinary outpourings of
the Holy Spirit on the people of their charge.

Affectionately yours,

PHOEBE PALMER

The following letter from *The Christian Guardian*, March 31, 1858,
was written by Rev. Samuel D. Rice and titled, "The Work of God in
Hamilton."

Mr. Editor,—The repugnance I have to write for publication must
be my excuse, (if any be needed,) for not communicating with
you at an earlier date, relative to the work of God in this city.
Discredit has been thrown on the work by some and exaggerated
by others. These conflicting rumors seem to demand a statement
of facts, and the more so, as some ministers have reported our
work here as valueless.

The work itself in power and extent for the time surpasses any
work I have seen in the course of my ministry—the efforts put
forth differ from any other.

The religious state of the Circuit, where I entered on my du-
ties here was good; evidences of salvation were obvious to those
who were disposed to consider the work. At the renewal of tick-
ets for the August quartet we had a membership of 500.

The Oakville Camp-meeting is so identified with our work
here that a passing remark concerning it seems necessary. When
the notice of it was published we urged our people to avail
themselves of the privilege of attending, and several joined in
preparing a Hamilton tent: several of those belonged to a praying
labouring band, who laid themselves out for promoting the work
of God. That Camp-meeting as you are aware became a Bethel,
and those attending from Hamilton shared largely in the blessings so freely dispensed.

While at the meeting I had invited Dr. and Mrs. Palmer to
pay me a visit, but absence from home at several of our autumn
camp-meetings had been so protracted that they deferred the acceptance of the invitation to a future time; but under a guidance
divine at the point of separation, they decided to stay a little with
us, and on Thursday evening they came to our city in company
with several from the Camp-ground. The design was formed to
test the principle of a "laity for the times." Each of us took a short

ramble, as we could find to meet with the Dr. and Mrs. Palmer at the Mc Nab-street church. This was our starting point.

There was a good attendance for the notice. Mrs. Palmer in her lucid and pointed manner, under such feelings as the Holy Spirit alone can produce, placed her thoughts before the company assembled—gave us an outline of a plan for personal effort, in the form of a home "camp-meeting," stating the state of heart necessary to engage successfully in such an enterprise. After stating the plan of personal effort clearly, time was given for consideration, and then each one willing to work was requested to give in his adhesion to the plan by rising. Most of those present arose and then came forward for special prayer for divine power and direction. God that night, accepted the sincerely offered devotion of his children's heart and labour, and from that private meeting, those who had pledged themselves for labour, went forth to fulfill their vows and redeem their pledges. The result was immediate. Attention to the great subject of personal salvation became apparent and scores night after night, presented themselves for prayer, and professed salvation. The plan of conducting the meetings was simple; one of ourselves stationed on the circuit opened the meeting and gave a short address. Mrs. Palmer followed, and Dr. Palmer invited seekers of salvation forward, while those who had been busy inviting persons during the day, looked after such in the meeting; thus all were at work, either in the prayer circle or in the congregation in true camp-meeting fashion.

The peculiar characteristic of the work was the ease and rapidity with which it moved. There was a great absence of external manifestations; the emotions were usually entirely under control, of the subjects of this work. I state this as a fact, not thereby expressing an opinion as to whether it was better or worse on this account.

Dr. and Mrs. Palmer, who are undoubtedly greatly honoured of God in their work, and whose labours in Canada have been incalculable service to us both directly and indirectly, and the results of whose labours cannot but remain when we shall have passed to the place of ultimate test. The Dr. and Mrs. Palmer remained with us a little over a fortnight after, and in that time and a fortnight after over 600 names were entered on our registry as saved. Some of those had been in the church; some were members—some from the country, and many from other churches in the city, for our meetings were not for proselytism but for salvations, and I doubt not that the registration was in the main a fair index of the results of four week's campaign. This result was reached by the united labours of the membership under the general direction of the above stated. We have had the opportunity of examining the work through two quarterly visitations and by personal pastoral converse. So far as these converts have become connected with us, or have belonged to the families of our people, and we have no hesitancy in saying that if the ordinary evidences that from the beginning have been recognized as valid, are to be relied on, then this work is truly the work of God, bearing His seal indubitably.

During the progress of the work which marked so many as "justified," a large number sought and found that "perfect love that casteth out fear," and are now "walking in the fear of the Lord and comfort of the Holy Ghost." These are numbered by scores, and clearly witnessed by a holy life that "the blood of Jesus Christ His Son, cleanseth them from all sin."

Monday evenings are given to the subject of Holiness, each minister on the circuit in his turn presiding. These meetings are more largely attended and possess a larger measure of divine power than any other of our week evening services. The number of our praying labouring band is increased, and not a week passes without the conversion or restoration of souls.

Those who are acquainted with the wear in our Societies in cities, and especially where want of work is added to commercial embarrassment, know well the need of constant revival to keep up numbers. It is with gratitude to God that we report the returns at the last quarterly visitation, after filling up the vacancies occurring through removal and otherwise, at 824. We did hope that we should be able to report the membership doubled, and we might, had united self-sacrificing labour been continued longer.

At the close of three week's labour we undertook the difficult work of forming the classes, and I feel it to be my duty to take a somewhat unusual course relative to the work, believing earnestly as I do in "revivals" and that without them Methodism would be shorn of her strength. I have been attacked on the reaction which frequently follows, and the diminution of numbers resulting. I have always been confident that the falling away has not been so much from the new members. If old members will pass through a season of grace, and not avail themselves of the opportunity to renew their strength, they grieve the Spirit of God, and we have known as a result some terrible back-sliding. Again, there are some leaders and some classes that have a wonderful facility for reducing their numbers, and you need a revival every year to keep such classes from becoming extinct; other classes are full and overflowing. The reason is obvious.

In our recent work we laid it down as a principle not to put the new converts into old classes. Only 80 for fear of convenience sake were put into the previously existing classes. We appointed new leaders, and made up the classes of new converts nearly doubling the number of leaders, so now we fairly test the statement that there is not so great defection in the members brought in by means of revival. So far the plan has succeeded better than we anticipated—the new classes are prosperous—good attendance of members and generally faithful.

The work in all its aspects is cheerful, and few churches owe a larger debt of gratitude to God than the Wesleyan Methodist Church in this city, and if the people called Methodists *will think, and plan, and risk, and sacrifice as much*—aye, a TITHE as much for church extension as for the secular advantages, then in this city we have prospects equal to any in this wide-world. I trust we shall know the day of visitation and improve it; a non-religious post teaches us what we ought now to ponder: "There is a tide in the affairs of men, which taken at the flood leads on to fortune."

The length of this communication is sufficient. I could not abbreviate it. With your leave there is another aspect of our work which, when I can get the time, I should like to present to your readers. In the meantime

I am, very truly,

Sam. D. Rice
Hamilton, March 16th, 1858

EXCERPTS FROM PHOEBE PALMER'S BOOK, PROMISE OF THE FATHER

This book was originally published in Boston by Henry V. Degen in 1859. The excerpts here are taken from the reprint by Schmul Rare Reprint Specialists of Salem Ohio, pages 251–65.

The following letter first appeared in *The Christian Advocate* 32, no. 45, November 5, 1857, page 185, addressed to Brother Dikeman in New York, under the title "Revival Extraordinary: The Laity for the Times Exemplified." The letter was dated Oct. 17, 1857, and the place was given as Hamilton C.W.

I have chosen to give excerpts of this letter from its later form in *The Promise of the Father* here rather than the version in *The Christian Advocate*. Although there are minor grammatical and punctuation changes in the book version, I believe that the later version uses simpler language. Both were written by Phoebe Palmer, although the *Christian Advocate* version was published closer to the actual time of the revival. Where there are important changes, the earlier *Christian Advocate* version is given in square brackets.

Hamilton, Canada West, October 17, 1857.

Rev.W.H.D.—

Dear Brother: What hath God wrought! Would that I could portray on paper the wonderful works of God, which we have witnessed in the last few days. It is now only a little over one week since we paused, with the intention of only tarrying for the night in this place. We were on our way homeward from one of the most glorious meetings we ever attended; and had the railroad cars favoured our purpose, we should have been with our New York friends one week yesterday.

But God's ways are not as our ways. We have witnessed, during the past twenty years, many signal displays of God's wonder-working power in saving souls, but never before have we witnessed a revival after this fashion; so remarkable in its aspects, so singularly suggestive and inspiring. The work began only a little over one week since, and already between three and four hundred have been brought into the fold of Christ. And still the work is going on with rapidly increasing power.

It is now Monday, October 19. It was only on Friday, one week since, that this glorious work commenced; twenty-one souls were blessed with pardon, and several others, I trust, with the full baptism of the Holy Ghost [sanctification], the first day that the extra effort commenced; since which the work has steadily increased in power, the number of the newly justified varying from twenty to forty-five each day, until yesterday, when, through Christ, the Captain of our salvation, over one hundred were won over to the ranks of the redeemed. Halleluia! The Lord God omnipotent reigneth! And let all the redeemed say, Amen, amen!

Thanks to the Lord of the harvest for such an in-gathering. And where will it end? Not, we trust, till all Canada is in a blaze. The work is taking within its range persons of all classes. Men of low degree, and men of high estate for wealth and position, old men and maidens, and even little children, are seen humbly kneeling together, pleading for grace. The mayor of the city, with other persons of like position are not ashamed to be seen bowed at the altar of prayer beside the humble servant, pleading for the full baptism of the Spirit [holiness]. My pen lingers. I might write a volume of interesting incidents, but I must forbear.

I commenced a letter, two or three days since, which I intended to have addressed to yourself, in connection with our dearly beloved pastor [Brother Roche]. In this I commenced to give, a little more in detail, a glance at our journeyings since we left New York. The recital would cheer your hearts amazingly; but time fails. Such are the exigencies of this glorious work that every moment has its demands. [I also commenced, several days ago to write a few lines in regards to our Canada tour for our excellent *Advocate*, (which, by the way, is really a great favorite with the Canadian Methodists) but failed with this, as with yours, for want of time.] But I must hasten. I have nearly filled my little sheet, yet in the multiplicity of good tidings have left unwritten that with which my pen was most heavily laden when I commenced to write. If the principle on which this revival *commenced*, and is now being carried out so wonderfully, is of God, where is there a place in God's dominions [where Christianity has the least foothold but may be] favored with a revival *at once?* This revival commenced, and is progressing, on precisely the principles laid down in the articles published in the Christian Advocate and Journal early last spring, under the caption, *"Laity for the times."*

Though Hamilton is favored with three devoted ministers, than whom few are more marked, in our own or any other church for [talent and pious and ministerial ability], eminent devotedness and ministerial ability, yet these ministers will be as free to acknowledge, to the praise of God, as ourselves, that this gust of divine power, now spreading as a pentecostal flame over this entire community, took its rise in the sudden rise of the *laity.*

In as few words as possible I will endeavor to tell you just how the work commenced; and then tell me whether the same principles, if brought into immediate requisition in all our New York churches, would not result in the salvation of thousands of souls in less than a week. The membership in Hamilton, comprising three Wesleyan churches, has heretofore numbered about five hundred. When we paused on our journey here, on Thursday last, one week since, with the expectation of tarrying but for the night, there was nothing in the tone of the meeting we attended which indicated the near approach of this extraordinary outpouring of the Spirit [gust of power].

It was the stated prayer meeting evening, and about seventy persons were present. We were led to speak of the solemn obligation of bringing *all* the tithes into the Lord's storehouse, in order that all the tithes of time, talent, and estate might be laid on God's holy altar, and thus be brought into immediate use, by way of saving a lost world. We suggested that if the people would pledge themselves thus to bring all the Lord's tithes into his storehouse at once, and go to work on the morrow to invite their neighbours to Christ, gracious results [a good result] might be seen the ensuing evening. Probably over thirty of those present raised their right hand in the presence of the Lord, in solemn affirmation that they would sacrifice that which cost them something, in earnest, specific endeavors to win souls to Christ.

A special meeting was appointed for the next evening. Each one had obligated himself to bring at least one with him, and to invite as many as possible. On coming together in the evening, the lecture room was found wholly insufficient to contain the people, and the large audience room was resorted to. Ministers had been alike diligent as the laity in giving sinners a personal invitation to come to Christ. The invitation had been accepted, and the glorious result of the first day's effort was that a score of souls were added to the ranks of the saved. And now the newly saved were pledged, in turn, to unite with those already in the field, in bringing their unsaved friends to Jesus. A meeting was appointed for the next afternoon and evening, and still the number doubled and trebled, till hundreds are now in daily attendance on the afternoon and evening meetings, and the revival seems to be the absorbing topic of all circles. And who can say where it will end? Think of the three or four hundred new recruits, and these all engaged alike with those before in the field, in daily renewal of efforts to bring one more.[*(footnote in the book version) *This, it will be remembered, was at the commencement of the great financial difficulties, and seems to have furnished data of the great revival which, as a pentecostal flame, has since been spreading over the American content.]

Nightly we pledged ourselves anew to bring yet one more the coming day; and thus the hosts of Zion are enlarging daily, and new cases are being ferreted out, which would never have been reached but by this system of vigorous daily effort. "Wonderful!" exclaimed one of aristocratic bearing, who had long been unapproachable on the subject of his soul's best interest. And now he had been approached by one who, having newly received the baptism of fire, feared [dared] to let him alone. The lady, who now dared to meet him in his own home, was one among the many scores who, with uplifted hand, was daily pledging herself to be "instant in season and out of season" in searching out some new subject for Christ's kingdom; and now, on being thus personally addressed, and beholding the tears of earnestness streaming from the eyes of the lady addressing him, he exclaimed with amazement, "Wonderful! What can this mean? Never did I see anything like it!" He listened with interest to expostulating tones of pious entreaty as they fell from the lips of the lady, and though he has not yielded to the claims of Christ, he has had a season of the Spirit's visitation, through human agency, without which the church might not have been clear of his blood, should he be lost.

Said another, who was a lady of some position, but who had long been a neglecter of salvation, "Why here is more than half a dozen different persons who have to-day been running to me on this subject. I do not see what has got into the people. Why, they must think that I am a dreadful sinner."

All classes are at work. Illustrations of exceeding interest come up before me; but I can scarcely trust myself to glance at them, they are so numerous and so suggestive [good]. Seldom have I seen a more lovely convert than one in the common walks of life. After her translation from the kingdom of darkness into the kingdom of God's dear Son, she was so entranced with the glory of the inheritance upon which she had just entered, that the utterances of her new-born Spirit were singularly beautiful and sublime. I mentioned this on my return to the family where we were entertained. "O, that is the one our Eliza brought," said our hostess. Eliza is a pious servant in the family, but, though pressed with an unusual amount of service just at this time, she had with others, lifted her hand by way of pledging herself to bring at least one.

"I did not know that our servant knew a person in the place, as we brought her from a distance, not very long since; but she had pledged herself to bring one, and that one was converted." So said the Rev. Mr. R., the minister who superintends the work here. The work is becoming the town topic. Men of business are after men of business; every man after his man. Surely this is a truthful demonstration of Christianity in earnest, and a return to what was said by an eminent divine of the more early Methodists— "They are all at it, and always at it."

In fact, it is only a return to primitive Christianity, when the manifestations of the Spirit were untrammeled by mere human opinions and church conventionalism, and permitted to have full sway. It is that which was foretold by the prophet Joel, and of which the apostle Peter spoke, when he proclaimed, "It shall come to pass, in the last days, saith God, I will pour out my Spirit upon all flesh, and your sons and your daughters shall prophesy; and on my servants and on my handmaidens I will pour out in those days of my Spirit, and they shall prophesy;" [etc.;] furnishing a marked demonstration that the same power still continues in the church that was in the apostolic church, when Saul, breathing out threatenings and slaughter, scattered the band of disciples, comprising men and women, in every direction. The infant church, with the exception of the apostles, were, by Saul's fearful havoc, scattered away from Jerusalem; and being thus scattered, these *men* and *women* of the laity went everywhere *preaching* the word. That is, they went abroad proclaiming the glad tidings of salvation, and urging the Gospel invitation.

And why may not all these instrumentalities again be brought into use? Have we not men, women, and children in our various churches, whose personal realizations of the blessedness of salvation empowers them to urge others to the gospel feast? O, will not the ministers of the sanctuary at once bring all these instrumentalities into action? Dormant power is in the church, which, if brought into immediate use, would result in the salvation of thousands speedily. Will not the captains of the hosts of Israel call upon the people to come up at once to the help of the Lord against the mighty? O, if we may only have a "laity for the times," how soon will this redeemed world be brought back to God! [pp. 251–58].

Phoebe Palmer

New York, November 14, 1857

To Rev. Mr. F—.

During the past summer and fall months we have been permitted to participate in more extraordinary out-pourings of the Spirit than we have ever before witnessed. Such exemplifications of the beauty and power of holiness, and such manifest effusions of grace in the awakening and conversion of sinners, we have seldom known.

I think that in the aggregate not less than two thousand souls have been converted. I would speak with carefulness before God, and I believe this to be a low computation. Hundreds of believers have also received the baptism of the Holy Ghost; and O, the power that has attended their ministrations! Would that I could describe the scenes of intense interest we have witnessed; and surely you would magnify God, and together we would exalt his name.

Our last visit was at London, C.W. While we were there a revival commenced, and many in the city of London and from the surrounding country were newly blest. The secretary of the meeting informed us that he had received about two hundred names. We remained with them twelve days, and when we left, the work was still most graciously progressing. A principle is involved in the progress of the remarkable revivals in which we have recently been engaged, we think singularly important, and which many in these regions are resolving to test. We are hearing of several encouraging things in connection with it. Companies of the laity are getting together and pledging themselves that they will go and do likewise. A lawyer, who is an earnest class-leader, told me a few hours since, that he took the paper containing the published account of the revival at Hamilton, and read it to the members of his class, instead of engaging in the usual exercise of relating experience. The result was, that the members united themselves into a band to carry out the principles of the letter. The revival in Hamilton is still going on, and at the last advices we were informed that between five and six hundred had been saved. The work of holiness is also going on with great power. While we were there, ministers and people were coming in from the country round about to share in the holy outpourings of grace. One man and his wife came seventy-five miles, seeking the full baptism of the Holy Spirit. The Lord fulfilled the desire of their hearts, and they returned to their home rejoicing with joy unspeakable and full of glory.

A letter lies unsealed before me, which I have just written to the Rev. Mr. R., which introduces a subject so dear to my heart, that I can scarcely forbear transcribing it for you. It stands in connection with the salvation of the perishing. This is one great work which above all others should occupy the attention of every professed servant of Christ.

"The Christian lives to Christ alone,
To Christ alone he dies."

It was the work of Christ to save the world. To the degree the disciple is Christ-like in his self-sacrificing efforts to save sinners, in a proportionate degree will he be made a partaker of Christ's joys. "That this my joy may be in them, and that their joy may be full." Christ's joy was to save the world, and bring many sons to glory. But I promised to give you my letter to the Rev. Mr. R., treating on this subject. And here it is:—

New York, November 13, 1857

To Rev. Mr. R—.

Dear Brother: It was near the midnight hour of October 30 that we parted with our London friends. Several brethren and sisters, dearly beloved in the Lord, accompanied us to the cars. There, at that affecting, solemn hour, we strengthened each other's hands in the Lord. Here, at the dead of night, we lingered at the depot about one hour, awaiting the "lightning train," which was to bear us to our distant home. We improved this hour of waiting in proposing plans for future conquests, which we hope may be as unending as eternity for good. As a company of God's sacramental hosts, we had just left a scene of triumph; and here, at this quiet hour, while the world was sleeping around us, we devised ways and means by which we might win the greatest possible number of souls to the Saviour. And here the whole company formed themselves into a band, which might be designated as a *"Soul-saving Band."* The company consisted of male and female followers of the Saviour. Some of these, though lovely and devoted, were timid and comparatively uninitiated in the arts of holy warfare. Others had, during the twelve days' campaign through which we had passed, endured hardness as good soldiers. Many scores, during the twelve days we had labored together in the city of L., enlisted under the Captain of our salvation; and now, as we were about parting, we memorialized the solemn hour by forming ourselves into a band, which we pray, may ever be signalized in the eye of God and man as a band of soul-savers. A board of direction was appointed, consisting of a presiding officer and a secretary, and the principles set forth in the accompanying preamble and resolutions were adopted. We send a copy of them to you, hoping that they may meet with your approval, and many may be induced to unite themselves in sustaining this, the most glorious enterprise that ever engaged the attention of a redeemed race. "Union is strength." And if the matter is of God, I trust many of our dear Hamilton friends will be induced to form themselves into the bands for this glorious purpose. As we passed through P.H., early in June last, similar bands were formed, and we found a letter awaiting our arrival home last week, giving an inspiring account of numbers who had been converted, and others wholly sanctified, through the energetic and unwearied efforts of the numbers of these bands.

BANDS OF SOUL-SAVERS.

The object of those whose names are hereunto annexed shall be to use every possible means, in their individual and collective capacity, to pluck sinners as brands from the burning.

And whereas purposes, however piously formed, or strongly made, are too often failures, unless means be ordained whereby they may be made an ever-present specialty;

And whereas the value of the soul outweighs all human considerations, and is an objective to which all business or domestic avocations should be subservient and tributary;

And whereas we believe we cannot serve the Lord Christ more effectually, either by way of bringing an increase of grace into our own souls in thus *using* the grace given, or to the individual benefit of the human family at large, than by making daily specific efforts in rescuing souls from death, for whom Christ shed his precious blood; therefore,–

1. *Resolved,* That while we would not be unmindful of the divine injunction, "Diligent in business," we will, through the assistance of almighty grace, manifest our fervor of spirit by endeavoring to make every earthly consideration, whether it be secular business or domestic avocations, specifically subservient to the service of Christ.

2. *Resolved,* That we will endeavor to save at least ONE HALF HOUR DAILY, and more, if possible, in specific, direct efforts to win souls to Christ; and this, God being our helper, we will endeavor to do, though it may be at the cost of a more habitual carefulness in treasuring up time, or though it may cost something in acts of self-denial, by either rising earlier or sitting up later, or may involve the necessity of casting aside the enthusiastic doctrine that we are not to do good unless we feel free to it, or though the cost of *pecuniary* profit; repelling with righteous indignation the idea that *Christians* are not required to sacrifice that which cost them something.

3. *Resolved,* That we will make earnest and prayerful efforts to engage all who love our Lord Jesus Christ to unite in this, the most momentous and ennobling Christian enterprise that can command the attentions of a redeemed world; enlisting, as far as in us lies, the interest of all professed Christians, whether young or old, and irrespective of denomination, inasmuch as all professed Christians are called to be *workers together* with God in bringing a revolted world back to the world's Redeemer.

4. *Resolved,* That we will, as far as circumstances permit, meet together weekly, at such time and place as, by mutual agreement, shall be deemed most expedient; in order—First: To seek counsel of God, "who teacheth our hands to war and our fingers to fight," and through whom alone we can wage a successful warfare against the hosts of sin. Second: To

present cases demanding special prayer, to report conversions, or cases of hopeful interest, for mutual counsel, and especially for the encouragement of the weak and timid, in order that the graces of the Spirit, in the weakest believer, may be brought into continuous requisition, and thereby be continually multiplied, and thus the timid and weak in Zion become courageous and strong as David.

5. *Resolved*, That in places where there may be more bands than one, it be recommended that they unite monthly; and where convenient, that the minister of the church, or one or more of the ministers of the churches to which the bands belong, be invited to be present and preside. A secretary may also be appointed, whose duty it shall be to read the reports of the various bands, and be ready, if deemed expedient, to present an annual report in January of each year, when an anniversary may be held in case it be regarded by a majority of the members subservient to the cause.

In all of which we, the undersigned, do agree, and in pledge of the sustainment of which we do hereby, in the name and presence of God, affix our names [pp. 259–65].

EXCERPTS FROM THE CHRISTIAN ADVOCATE AND JOURNAL

The following, titled "The Revival," is taken from the *Christian Advocate and Journal* 33, no. 12, of 25 March, 1858, page 46.

In Progress—General Recognition —The Secular Press—Absence of Excitement—What was Immediate Occasion?—Activities of the Church—Non-evangelical Religious Sentiment— "Freeman's Journal"—"Churchmen"—The Universalists—Dr. Bellows—Conclusions.

The revival of religion, of which we have given some account in former numbers, still continues to spread on every side, and with more and more remarkable manifestations of power. To record a tithe of the highly interesting revival intelligence which comes to our hands, just such, too, as ordinarily we would eagerly lay hold of, would occupy most of our columns from week to week. We are therefore compelled, by sheer necessity, to omit nearly everything in the form of details and local incidents, and to confine our remarks to less interesting, but more comprehensive, general statements and reflections. In the appropriate department will be found a condensed summary of revival intelligence, sent us from various places, but these though highly valuable, give no adequate notion of the wide-spread influence of this work. Its progress seems like the march of a conqueror, and its presence is like the breath of spring, all-pervading and life-giving. It reaches from the ocean to the Western frontier, and cities, towns and country are alike affected by it; and though it has already continued more than three months, it shows no signs of abatement. A striking evidence of the influence of this work is its general recognition beyond merely religious circles. Everybody speaks of the "great awakening" as a well ascertained fact. The secular press, in all parts of the country, chronicles its progress as an important item of local intelligence. Newspaper correspondents write of it in their communications, in common with finances, politics, and the weather; and the telegraph is brought into requisition to convey the news of the triumphs of the Gospel from city to city. These things indicate an unusual state of the public mind, and show that it is very widely and powerfully affected. Though less strongly marked in some of its features than former similar visitations, all agree that in extent, and in its hopeful results, the present revival exceeds any with which the American Churches have been favored during the last half century.

The degree of attention, devoted to this matter by the secular press, great as it confessedly is, is less remarkable than the tone and spirit in which the subject is treated. Experience has accustomed us to expect from much of the non-religious press of all grades, when the subject is not systematically ignored, either the most apathetic recognition of vital religion, or sneers at the "fanaticism" of its professors, or a kind of patronizing and half-way apologetical confession of some of its incidentally beneficial results. We have been so long used to this state of things that we have learned to expect it as a matter of course, so that this change of tone awakens a more lively interest. But the press is only a reflection of the public sentiment, and therefore we may, from its utterances, infer a great and most salutary reaction in the public mind on this subject. Probably the favorable feeling toward the work of religion evinced by the press, may be attributed somewhat to some of the peculiarities of this revival. Generally all strongly marked excitements in matters of religion are offensive to irreligious persons. This is natural. Men are always displeased with exhibitions of emotions with which they cannot sympathize, and especially when they are opposed to their preconceived notions. And as this revival is distinguished for the absence of all strong exhibitions of feeling, whether joyful or otherwise, this cause of offense is taken away; perhaps, too, a more honorable cause may have aided to producing this result. The public sentiment of the country is doubtless becoming more Christianized, and is really less hostile to true religion than formerly; nor should we wholly exclude, in this particular, the operation of an agency by which the hearts of the children of men are turned as the rivers of waters. In the last and triumphant conflict of the Church against sin, the world shall be on the side of the taught; and what if even not this shall be somewhat the case?

This absence of excitement is indeed among the most remarkable features of this revival. In all former cases of the kind, among whatever denominations of Christians they may have occurred, strong emotions have attended the progress of religious awakenings. These excitements have indeed presented widely different aspects, according to the various characters of individuals and the different usages of Churches; but generally the power of the spirit of revival has been pretty fairly indicated by the degree of emotion manifested. Not so, however, in this case. That there has been a quickening of the religious feelings of the Churches, and an increase of evangelical efforts, is not to be denied, though it is equally certain that at scarcely any other period has there been less of that kind of religious fervor, which tends to fanaticism. In the midst of the most striking displays of Divine power, there is a wonderful calmness and even coolness among both the actors and subjects of the revival. Christians converse among themselves of the deep things of the Spirit, or with the unconverted of the necessity of conversion, with a quietness such as has not before been witnessed; and persons become awakened, set out to seek religion, and pass through all the stages of repentance and conversion, with a sober self-possession as pleasing as it is unprecedented. For the explanation of this state of facts we have no theory to offer. We are fully persuaded that the whole work is eminently of the agency of the Holy Spirit, and that he orders its operations according to his own sovereign purposes.

People very naturally ask for the cause why this great work has come at this time, rather than at any other; and in this question it is often assumed, to an extent that we are not prepared to allow, that the Spirit's operations are dependent on certain instrumental agencies. Doubtless the Spirit works through instrumentalities, but his chief instruments are the ordinances of the Church. It may also be conceded that the piety and zeal of Christians hold an important relation to the efficiency of the Divine grace, though not such as to render the work of the Spirit wholly dependent on human fidelity. That the Divine providence may prepare the way for the Spirit is certain, but the ways of the Divine hand are beyond our understanding, and cannot be made the basis of a calculation. It is quite probable that the late financial crisis has in some cases been overruled to the spiritual benefit of its victims; but there have been similar revulsions in financial affairs, which were not followed by such consequences. God's ways are not as our ways. He can make the most trifling event the occasion for the most wonderful changes, because in all cases the efficiency is in himself. We may apply the figure of the wind blowing as it listeth to the process of the Spirit in a general revival of religion, as well as in the conversion of an individual soul.

We have been not a little interested in the discussions of this subject by those who may be called outsiders and lookers on. The merely non-religious press very generally, though not universally, treat it fairly and with a commendable deference. We presume, too, that in most cases their disqualifications are made in all sincerity, though the stand-point of the writers may be somewhat fictitious. In the editorial corps of our principal papers are a considerable number of pious and truly evangelical Christians, and a still larger share among their editorial contributors. This may in part account for the character of these discussions, but they have a deeper significance than all this. Newspaper publishers who live by the favor of the public, feel it to their interest to offer no violence to the religious sentiment of the people; and they have sufficiently ascertained what that sentiment is, to forbid them to trifle with these manifestations of spiritual religion. Evangelical Christianity is both a conviction and a sentiment with our governing masses, and none who value their favor can afford to indulge in profane jests at its expense. There is, in fact, a sensitiveness. In this matter, which, though we do not wholly approve of it, renders them less tolerant of open infidelity than of many forms of immorality.

Within a very few years past a great change has taken place in the attitude of certain parties of great influence towards Christianity. It is not very long ago that a kind of godless humanitarianism was threatening to supersede the Gospel, and bring in a new evangel of universal good-will, without requiring the painful self-abnegation which Christianity demands. Around this the secular philosophy of the age rallied itself, and many a bitter taunt was uttered against the church, for neglecting men's real wants to care for the imaginary ones of their souls. This insidions attack was met and repelled by the church, less indeed by learned controversy than by the strife of good works, til every honest friend of his race has been compelled, by the act of charities of the church, to confess the supreme excellence of Christianity over every other form of beneficence. The progress of this change in the public sentiment, at least in a very considerable portion of society, is well illustrated in the history and the changing attitudes of the *New York Tribune*, in its relations to evangelical Christianity. Setting out with an honest purpose to promote the best interest of society, but without any fixed religious convictions, the governing mind of that most powerful organ of public opinion has been steadily advancing nearer and near to the stand-point of Christianity, as embodied and brought into action in the evangelical Churches of the country. The active charities of the Church have gained for her, and for the great truths of the Gospel, an honorable standing among all men of real goodness of character. By these "good works" the great head of the church seeks to be glorified among men, and through their instrumentality the Gospel is to win its way to universal acceptance. The well defined position of the Church relative to the great moral questions involved in the conflicts of the times is no doubt contributing largely to her moral power. The sneers and insults which have been cast upon venerable and unassuming ministers of the Gospel, by men in high places, have not been unheeded by an intelligent people; and in the position thus assumed for the Church by her ministers, she commands the public conscience, though she may gain the reproaches of those whose interest she damages. Never, probably, has the enlightened conscience of the American people more fully sympathized with their ministers than they do at this very time; and the moral power thus given to them, and exerted by them in their ministrations, is now receiving its highest commendations in the manifest presence and saving power of the Holy Spirit.

The religious press has of course spoken out on this subject, generally, as would be presumed, in language of thanksgiving and exultant praise. But in this almost perfect harmony a few faint discords are heard. The organ of Romish archepiscopate is of course quite out of tune, since it well knows that whatever is gained to vital religion is lost to *its* formalism. But never before, perhaps, has the position of Romanism in any community so exactly answered to Bunyan's picture of the giant "pope," sitting at the door of his cave and biting his nails, as the pilgrim passed by him in safety. Nothing else is so certainly fatal to all false religions, as a genuine revival of the truth; and in no other way may we so surely guard against the inroads of the papal sect as by the propagation of pure and spiritual Christianity. We have been pained to find the carpings of the archbishop's "Journal" seconded by a paper clasped among the Protestant publications; but, as we have heretofore shown by extracts from the *Churchman*, it appears that that sheet is scarcely less scandalized by what it sees going forward among the "sects," than is its popish *confrere*. But we are pleased to know that print expresses the sentiments of only an inconsiderable portion of the great and highly respectable Protestant Episcopal Church in this city; a Church which is sharing to some good degree in the present gracious revival, as well as contributing, especially through the laity, to its promotion. The *"Protestant Churchman,"* the organ of the more evangelical party, is heartily in sympathy with the good work.

It is not a little strange, and would be something specially remarkable, had not strange things ceased to elicit remark, that the Universalists of this city and vicinity seem to be well affected toward the revival, and to some extent they are cooperating with the movement. Rev. Mr. Peters, pastor of the Universalist Church in Brooklyn, (Williamsburg,) lately made the revival the subject of a sermon, in which he admitted both the need of a religious awakening in the community, and his confident hope that the present excitement would result in great and permanent religious benefits. Rev. Dr. Sawyer, of this city, has evinced a very decided sympathy with the prevailing religious interest, in which he is seconded by some of his principal laymen; and among the numerous announcements for special prayer-meetings is that of one to be held in his church on Wednesday and Friday evenings. These are indeed strange things, and almost allow the hope that some good may yet come out of these non-evangelical bodies. Hereafter sneers of the professors of that form of faith (if faith it may be called) at the practices of evangelical Christians, will be effectually stopped, since the examples of its great leaders may be challenged in their favor.

We intended, when we commenced this sketch of the progress of this great work, to pay our respect to our old friend, Dr. Bellows, of All-Souls, who has spoken out on the occasion, and, with the characteristic irreligion and politeness, undertaken to pronounce judgment on the whole affair. Dr. B. thinks the revival a good thing for those among whom it operates, as "an irrepressible outburst of pent-up religious feeling, which had found no life in the faulty theology and dead teachings of those who should have been its religious teachers." But for Unitarians he thinks nothing of the sort is needed; and so they are exhorted to "look down from the serene heights of their moral vantage-ground upon this and all excitements," and not to desire its influences, since they always have that which is more excellent. All this, and the much more of the same kind, with which the discourse quoted from abounds, is quite in character, and would be very ludicrous, on account of its absurdity, were it not too serious a subject to justify such a treatment. We hope at another time to examine this subject more fully than we can now do, with immediate references to the objections raised by a class of minds whom Dr. Bellows attempts to represent; although he evidently fails to appreciate their honest difficulties, and is quite incapable of sympathizing with their earnest longings, both for a solution of their doubts and for more adequate answering to their spiritual aspirations.

In conclusion, we congratulate our readers and the whole church in view of this gracious visitation of the Spirit. "The Lord has done great things for us, whereof we are glad." It is both our right and our duty to rejoice and give praise. But let us also remember that we are still in the heat of the conflict, and there is yet very much to be done before the powers of sin shall be overthrown, and the reign of Christ becomes universal. Now is the time for Christian efforts, individual as well as associated, for the salvation of souls. Let parents bring their children to Christ in prayer, and by placing them within the influences of the Church. Let friends solicit friends to go up to the house of the Lord, or directly call on them and urge them to become Christians. Let preachers, while guarding the excitement against abuses, seek to spread it wider and further. Never were such efforts more certain of success than just now; let us work while it is called to-day, for the night cometh when no man can work.

OBITUARIES

Mrs. E. A. Boice

This was originally published in *The Christian Guardian*, August 6, 1890 under the heading "The Righteous Dead."

Mrs. E. A. Boice was born April, 1814, at Derry Vermont. Her parents were originally Presbyterians, but afterwards they joined the Methodist Church, when residing in the township of Hallowell, county Prince Edward, Ontario. She was converted when eleven years of age, largely through the instrumentality of her sister Mary, who passed away to the better world when eighteen years of age. She was baptized by Elder Case [?- the print is unclear on the microfilm]. When seventeen years of age she moved to Picton to school, where she remained until twenty years of age. During the first year of her stay there occurred, perhaps, the greatest revival of religion with which Picton was ever visited, and then she entered into a life fully commemorated to God, and lived this life for nearly fifty-nine years, until death sealed her testimony. She taught school in Hillier for six months and in Picton for three months, making her home with Rev. John Ryerson. At the end of that time she came up to Dundas and kept house for her brother, Mr. John T. Larkin. In November, 1836, she was united in marriage to Mr. Wm Boice. In the spring of 1838 they moved to Hamilton, where Mr. Boice entered into mercantile business. In May, 1840, they moved to Picton, where their two eldest children, John and Mary, were born. Four years after they returned to Hamilton, where Mr. Boice entered into partnership with Mr. Larkin. During her first stay in Hamilton, in 1838, she joined the King Street Methodist church—the only one then open—under the pastorate of Rev. John Davidson, and on their return to this city she again united with the same church under Rev. Lewis Warner. In 1848 they again removed to Dundas, where they remained until the death of her brother, in 1851, when they once more returned to Hamilton, where Mr. Boice remained in business until 1871. In March, 1852, during the memorable revival, under Rev. James Caughey (the Revs. John Carroll and E. B. Harper being pastors), she first enjoyed the blessings of a holy heart. She was appointed class leader in the MacNab Street church, an office which she held for nearly twenty years. Under her leadership the class made rapid progress.

In October, 1859, she was instrumental in inducing the well-known and devoted evangelists Dr. and Mrs. Palmer, to remain in Hamilton for two weeks as her guests, during which time a memorable work of grace broke out in the city, which added largely to the membership of the three churches. It was at this time that Mr. Boice became more fully consecrated, and was appointed class-leader, which position he held until December, 1870, when he was stricken down with paralysis. The memory of this time of blessing was always a great source of comfort and delight to Mrs. Boice. She was called to pass through many and severe afflictions. Her health was not good. Even in her school-days there were tokens of physical impairment. In later years, when her husband was away in Europe, and four children about her, she was taken with alarming symptoms. She took her case to God in prayer; and received such a blessing for body and soul that in a short time her trouble was all gone, and she was able once more to take up life's work. Her vitality was very great. Often in later years she would be brought near to death's door

and lifted up again. In the midst of all her affliction, she bore up with amazing patience and fortitude. In early life she suffered the loss of parents and of a dear sister; then of an only brother; and further a great affliction in the loss of her only daughter, Mary in December, 1862; then the severest blow, when her noble husband became paralyzed. For years she helped to nurse him and was his constant and faithful companion. His death in 1879 left her a widow indeed—daughter taken, sons away from her, husband gone; but amid it all, God abundantly sustained her. She was of a lively, vivacious spirit. In her younger days she was leader in all cheerful, innocent pleasures, and in later life added much to the charm of social life. She was a woman of great energy. Her spirit sustained her under many heavy burdens, when the body seemingly was too weak to bear the strain. Her piety was earnest and hopeful. She loved the means of grace, prized the Word of God and fellowship with his people, and was an earnest and most successful worker in the Church. Through all her prolonged attacks of sickness she was conscious of the presence and grace of God. We are confident she is now rejoicing with husband and daughter in the presence of the glorified above.
   —*Hamilton Evening Times*, June 23rd, 1890.

Notes: This obituary was published first in the *Hamilton Evening Times* and was reprinted in the *Christian Guardian*. Mrs. Boice was a part of the original Methodist churches in Hamilton. Her obituary refers to the fact that she had experienced revival twice, once under James Caughey and once under the Palmers (date was clearly wrong for the Palmer's October visit). She was a class leader of the MacNab Street church when the Palmers came to visit. It is unclear what was meant that the Palmers were her guests. Did it mean that they were her house guests or guests of her church? Mrs. Boice's life was full of trials, but she leaned on God for support and experienced grace in the midst of them.

John Francis Moore (1857 Hamilton Mayor)

This was published in the *Hamilton Spectator*, April 7, 1870.

Death of Mr. John Francis Moore.—We learn from Montreal that the above named gentlemen died in that city on Tuesday last. Mr. Moore was an old citizen of Hamilton,—which he left but a few years ago—having settled here when it was but a village.—Some twenty-seven years ago Mr. Moore, in company with his brother, kept a large grocery store on the south side of the market square.

On the town becoming incorporated Mr. Moore became one of the representatives of St. Lawrence Ward in the Council, and he continued to sit in the Council as Alderman till 1858, in which year he was chosen Mayor. Mr. Moore was the first that adopted the system of borrowing money by debentures. His first venture was $20,000 for a complete system of sewerage. He also inaugurated the water works, both of which undertakings have been a standing credit to the city. Mr. Moore was one of the few that built the John Street Methodist Church, and he was one of the trustees of the church till he left the city to reside in Montreal. He was a native of Wiltshire, England. His remains will arrive this (Thursday) evening, and the funeral takes place from the residence of his son in-law, Mr. James Williamson, Ferguson avenue, on Friday morning, at 10 oclock.—We understand the City Council will attend the funeral in a body.

Notes: The date of Mr. John Moore's appointment as mayor of Hamilton is given incorrectly in his obituary. The City of Hamilton website as well as other sources list him as the mayor in 1857. According to the *Dictionary of Hamilton Biography*, John Moore proclaimed a day of "humiliation and prayer" following the train accident known as the Desjardins Canal Disaster that occurred on March 12, 1857.

Bibliography

ARCHIVES

UCA = United Church Archives, Toronto, Ontario
FPUCA = First-Pilgrim United Church Archives, Hamilton, Ontario
HPLA = Hamilton Public Library Archives, Hamilton, Ontario

PRIMARY SOURCES

Bradbury, William. *The New Golden Trio: "New Golden Chain," "New Golden Shower" and "New Golden Censer."* New York: William B. Bradbury, 1866. Online: http://books.google.ca/books?id=vWwVAAAAYAAJ&printsec=frontcover&source=gbs_ge_summary_r&cad=0#v=onepage&q&f=false (accessed December 17, 2014).
Census of the Canadas 1851–1852. Personal Census. Quebec: John Lovell, 1853.
Census of the Canadas 1860–1861. Quebec: Printed by S. B. Foote, 1863.
"Current Topics and Events: Death of Rev. Rice." *Canadian Methodist Magazine* 21, no. 2 (1885) 178–81.
"Dedication: Opening of the New Wesleyan Methodist Church, King Street East." *The Hamilton Spectator*, Thursday February 18, 1869, 1.
Dewart, E. H. "Samuel Dwight Rice." *The Christian Guardian*, December 17, 1884, 420.
"The Financial Crisis." *New York Times*, October 14, 1857, 1.
"The Financial Panic." *New York Times*, September 14, 1857, 4:3–4.
"Fine Record of Wesley." *Christian Herald*, March 19, 1909. Microfilm accessed through HPLA Local History & Archives, Reference Collection: Hamilton Collection. Vol. C4.4. Churches, Methodist.
"The Great Utility of Camp Meetings in Promoting Revivals of Religion." *Christian Guardian*, October 31, 1832, 201.
Hamilton Wesleyan Methodist Circuit Records, UCA.
Moody, D. L. *To The Work! To The Work! Exhortations to Christians.* New York: Fleming H. Revell, 1884. Online: http://babel.hathitrust.org/cgi/pt?q1=men%20and%20women%20of%20average%20talent;id=nyp.33433068288384;view=1up;seq=93;start=1;sz=10;page=search;num=87#view=1up;seq=88
"Mount Elgin Industrial Institute." The Children Remembered: Residential School Archive Project. UCA. Online: http://thechildrenremembered.ca/schools-history/mount-elgin/.
"The Ontario Provincial Exhibition." *The Globe*, September 25, 1847, 2. Online: http://search.proquest.com/docview/1507560561?accountid=47516

Palmer, Phoebe. "A Revival after Apostolic Times." *The Christian Guardian*, December 2, 1857, 1. Microfilm accessed at UCA.

—. *Promise of the Father*. Boston: Henry V. Degen, 1859. Repr. Salem, OH: Schmul Rare Reprint Specialists.

Prime, Samuel Irenaeus. *The Power of Prayer: Illustrated in the Wonderful Displays of Divine Grace at the Fulton Street and Other Meetings in New York and Elsewhere in 1857 and 1858*. New and Enlarged ed. New York: Scribner, Armstrong & Co., 1873. Online: https://archive.org/details/powerofprayerillwdooprim

"The Revival." *The Christian Advocate and Journal* 32, no. 12, March 25, 1858, 46. Microfilm accessed at UCA.

Rice, Samuel D. "The Work of God in Hamilton." *The Christian Guardian*, March 31, 1858, 2. Microfilm accessed at periodical collection Mills Library, McMaster University in Hamilton, ON, and UCA.

"The Righteous Dead." *The Christian Guardian*, August 6, 1890, 491. Microfilm accessed at periodical collection, Mills Library, McMaster University in Hamilton, ON.

Shephard, William A. *1858 City of Hamilton Directory*. Hamilton, ON: The Christian Advocate Printing House, 1858.

Sutherland, James. *1869 City of Hamilton Directory*. HPLA [no additional information was available on microfilm or in print, as the Archives had old worn copies of this book.]

Warner, Anna Bartlett, and Susan Warner. *Say and Seal Volume II*. Philadelphia: J. B. Lippincott, 1860. Available online: http://books.google.ca/books?id=GRAXBc KQEnUC&printsec=frontcover#v=onepage&q=jesus%20loves%20me&f=false (accessed December 17, 2014).

"Wesley United Church (Hamilton, Ont) Fonds." UCA. Fonds 1357.

"Why There Is No More Revival." *Canada Christian Advocate* 13, no. 42. October 17, 1857, 2, col. 2. Hamilton, ON. Microfilm accessed at periodical collection, Mills Library, McMaster University, Hamilton, ON.

"Zion Tabernacle Sunday School, Zion United Church Scrapbook." Vol. 1, 1894 – HPLA.

SECONDARY SOURCES

Airhart, Phyllis D. *Serving the Present Age: Revivalisim, Progressivism and the Methodist Tradition in Canada*. Montreal and Kingston: McGill-Queen's University Press, 1992.

Bailey, Thomas Melville, ed. *Dictionary of Hamilton Biography*. Vol. 1. Hamilton, ON: Ontario Heritage Foundation, Ministry of Culture and Recreation, and the Regional Municipality of Hamilton-Wentworth, 1912.

Baldwin, Laura. "City's Wesley United Church Counts History back to '78." *Hamilton Daily News*, October 15, 1955, 10. [The *Hamilton Daily News*, also called the *Hamilton News*, was published from 1947 to 1956 and can be accessed at HPLA.]

Bellamy, Margret (designer), and Warren Riley (photographer). *St. Paul's Church: James St. & Jackson St. Hamilton, Ontario Heritage Building*. Hamilton, ON. Privately Published.

Bush, Peter George. "James Caughey, Phoebe and Walter Palmer and the Methodist Revival Experience in Canada West 1850–1858." MA thesis. Queen's University, 1985.

The Centenary Story: Centenary United Church, 24 Main St. at MacNab. Hamilton, ON. Privately Published. August 18, 2007. Online: http://www.centenaryunited.org/history-2/the-centenary-story/ (accessed June 2013).

Centennial of Wesley United Church, Hamilton ON 1839 to 1939. Hamilton, ON. FPUCA and HPLA, [1939?].

Carroll, John. "Rev. E. B. Harper: The Conference and the Crayons: Crayon Seventeenth." In *Past and Present, or, a Description of Persons and Events Connected with Canadian Methodism for the Last Forty Years*, 267–68. Alfred Dredge: Toronto, 1860.

Carwardine, Richard. *Transatlantic Revivalism: Popular Evangelicalism in Britain and America, 1790–1865*. Westport, CN: Greenwood, 1978.

Challies, Tim. "Hymn Stories: Stand Up, Stand Up for Jesus." Posted June 30, 2013. Online: http://www.challies.com/articles/hymn-stories-stand-up-stand-up-for-jesus (accessed October 22, 2013).

Chapman, Wilbur. *The Life and Work of D. L. Moody*. Philadelphia: Universal, 1900. Online: https://archive.org/stream/lifeworkofdwightoochap#page/no/mode/2up (accessed December 18, 2014).

Chicago Historical Society. "The Great Chicago Fire." Online: http://www.chicagohs.org/history/fire.html (accessed December 17, 2014).

City of Hamilton History. HPLA Card Collection, 2013.

City of Hamilton Population. HPLA Card Collection, 2013.

Clayton, Cal. "Joseph Scriven 1819–1886." Port Hope, ON. Online: http://www.porthopehistory.com/jmscriven/josephscriven.htm (accessed December 18, 2014).

Cleland, James. *What a Friend We Have in Jesus: And Other Hymns by Joseph Scriven*. Port Hope, ON: W. Williamson, 1895.

Davis, Calvin. *Centennial Souvenir of First Methodist Church, Hamilton, Ontario, Canada 1821:1924*. Hamilton, ON: Centennial Committe under the Authority of the Official Board of the Church, 1924.

Dayton, Lucille Sider, and Donald W. Dayton. "'Your Daughters Shall Prophesy': Feminism in the Holiness Movement." *Methodist History* 14 (1978) 67–92.

Deen, Edith. *All the Women of the Bible*. New York: Harper & Row, 1988.

Fayter, Paul. Interview with Sandra King, June 17, 2013. Paul Fayter is a former minister of First-Pilgrim United Church, Hamilton, Ontario, and a historian.

Gray, Christopher. "Streetscapes/Fulton Street between Nassau and Williams Streets: A Vibrant and Noisy Block with Varied Architecture." *New York Times*, January 12, 2003, Real Estate Section. http://www.nytimes.com/2003/01/12/realestate/streetscapes-fulton-street-between-nassau-williams-streets-vibrant-noisy-block.html.

Henley, Brian. *1846 Hamilton: From a Frontier Town to the Ambitious City*. Burlington, ON: North Shore, 1995.

———. Interview with Sandra King, December 12, 2006. Retired Local History Librarian, Hamilton Public Library.

James, William. "Hamilton's Old Pumphouse." Posted December 03, 1998. Online: http://www.soe.uoguelph.ca/webfiles/wjames/homepage/Teaching/HamiltonsOldPumpHouse.htm.

Long, Kathryn T. *Revival of 1857–58: Interpreting an American Religious Awakening*. Religion in America Series. New York: Oxford University Press, 1998.

Merseyside Maritime Museum. "Information Sheet 64." Online: http://www.liverpoolmuseums.org.uk/maritime/archive/sheet/64.

McGregor-Clewes, Mary. "Peden, Rev Robert." Posted April 10, 1999 on Ancestry.com.   Online: http://archiver.rootsweb.ancestry.com/th/read/ PEDEN/1999–04/0923756927 (accessed October 29, 2013).

Moody, William R. *The Life of Dwight L. Moody*. New York: Fleming H. Revell, 1900. Online: https://archive.org/stream/cu31924029358961#page/no/mode/2up (accessed December 17, 2014).

Oden, Thomas C., ed. *Phoebe Palmer: Selected Writings*. Mahwah, NJ: Paulist, 1988.

Orr, J. Edwin. *The Second Evangelical Awakening*. London: Lowe & Brydone, 1949. Repr. Fort Washington, PA: Christian Literature Crusade, 1964.

Orr, J. Edwin, and Richard Owen Roberts, eds. *The Event of the Century: The 1857–1858 Awakening*. Wheaton, IL: International Awakening, 1989.

Owensby, Gillian. Sermon. Hamilton Christian Fellowship, Hamilton, Ontario, June 9, 2013.

Pawson, Ralph. *Growing Together: A History of First-Pilgrim United Church, Hamilton, Ontario*. Privately Printed, 1998.

The Pilgrim's Guide to Christ Church Cathedral: Hamilton, Ontario, Canada. Pamphlet. Hamilton, ON [n.d.].

Port Hope Scriven Committee. "Joseph Scriven." Online: http://www.josephscriven.org/ Home/Scriven_Bio.html (accessed December 18, 2014).

Raser, Harold E. *Phoebe Palmer: Her Life and Thought*. Lewiston, NY: Edwin Mellen, 1947.

"Revivals that Changed a Nation: A Conversation with Nathan O. Hatch." *Christian History* Issue 45, vol. 14, no. 1 (1995) 44. Online: http://www.christianitytoday. com/ch/1995/issue45/4542.html.

Rodrigue, Jean-Paul. "The Geography of Transport Systems." Online: https://people. hofstra.edu/geotrans/eng/ch3en/conc3en/linertransatlantic.html.

Ruggle, Richard E. "Booker, Alfred." *Dictionary of Canadian Biography*. Vol. 3, *1851– 1860*. University of Toronto. Online: http://www.biographi.ca/en/bio/booker_ alfred_1800_57_8E.html (accessed November 5, 2013).

Semple, Neil. *The Lord's Dominion: The History of Canadian Methodism*. Montreal and Kingston: McGill-Queen's University Press, 1996.

Shelley, Bruce L. *Church History in Plain Language*. Dallas: Word, 1982.

Smith, Timothy L. *Revivalism and Social Reform: American Protestantism on the Eve of the Civil War*. New York: Harper & Row, 1975.

"Today in History: August 24. The Panic of 1857." The Library of Congress: American Memory, Washington DC. Online: http://memory.loc.gov/ammem/today/aug24. html (accessed December 17, 2014).

Towns, Elmer. L., and Douglas Porter. *The Ten Greatest Revivals Ever: From Pentecost to the Present*. Ann Arbor, MI: Vine, 2000.

Turcotte, Dorothy, and Jean Jarvis. *Greetings from Grimsby Park: The Chautauqua of Canada*. Grimsby, ON: Grimsby Historical Society, 1985.

Van Die, Marguerite. *An Evangelical Mind: Nathanael Burwash and the Methodist Tradition in Canada, 1839–1918*. Montreal and Kingston: McGill-Queen's University Press, 1989.

Watson, Milton, and Charles MacDonald. *The History of Hamilton and District*. Edited by Milton Watson. Hamilton, ON: Hamilton Wentworth Board of Education, 1974.

Weaver, John C. *Hamilton: An Illustrated History*. Toronto: J. Lorimer, 1982.

Welcome to Christ's Church (Anglican) Cathedral. Hamilton, ON. Flyer [n.d.].

Wesley Urban Ministries. "Our History" [n.d.]. Online: http://www.wesleyurbanministries.com/index.php?page=history (accessed October 23, 2013).

Westfall, William. *Two Worlds: The Protestant Culture of Nineteenth Century Ontario.* Montreal and Kingston: McGill-Queen's University Press, 1990.

Wheatley, Richard. *The Life and Letters of Mrs. Phoebe Palmer.* New York: W. C. Palmer, Jr., 1876. [I worked from the 1984 reproduction of the 1881 reprint, produced by Garland in New York.]

White, Charles Edward. *The Beauty of Holiness: Phoebe Palmer as Theologian, Revivalist, Feminist and Humanitarian.* Grand Rapids: Zondervan, 1986.

Whiteley, Marilyn Färdig. *Canadian Methodist Women, 1766–1925: Marys, Marthas, Mothers in Israel.* Studies in Women and Religion. Waterloo, ON: Wilfrid Laurier University Press, 2005.

Wilkinson, Charles. "Great Awakening Began in Hamilton." *Hamilton Spectator*, October 17, 1981, 18.

"The Wrecking Crew: They Made Short Work of Historic Landmark." *Hamilton Spectator*, March 8, 1975, 26.

ADDITIONAL RESOURCES FOR FURTHER STUDY

Carroll, John. "Rev. S. D. Rice: The Conference and the Crayons: Crayon Fourth." In *Past and Present, or, Description of Persons and Events Connected with Canadian Methodism for the Last Forty Years*, 247–48. Alfred Dredge: Toronto, 1860.

"Dwight L. Moody." In *131 Christians Everyone Should Know*, edited by Mark Galli and Ted Olsen, 70–72. Nashville: Broadman & Holdman, 2000. Online: http://www.christianitytoday.com/ch/131christians/evangelistsandapologists/moody.html (accessed October 21, 2013).

"First Methodist Church, Hamilton." Pamphlet. FPUCA [n.d].

Heath, A. Elaine. *Naked Faith: The Mystical Theology of Phoebe Palmer.* Princeton Theological Monograph Series. Eugene, OR: Wipf & Stock, 2009.

Hibberd, F. G. *Biography of Rev. Leonidas L. Hamline, Late One of the Bishops of the Methodist Episcopal Church.* Cincinnati, OH: Jennings & Pye, 1881.

Lucy, Eleanor. *A Short History of the Centenary United Church on the Occasion of the Downtown Hamilton Sesquicentennial Church Walkabout.* Pamphlet privately published, March 1996.

Macpherson, Jay. "Scriven, Joseph Medlicott." In *Dictionary of Canadian Biography.* Vol. 11. University of Toronto/Université Laval, 2003–. Online: http://www.biographi.ca/en/bio/scriven_joseph_medlicott_11E.html (accessed December 18, 2014).

Palmer, Walter C., ed. *Life and Letters of Leonidas L. Hamline, D.D.* New York: Nelson & Phillips, 1866.

Rayburn, Alan. *Naming Canada: Stories about Places from Canadian Geographic.* Toronto: University of Toronto Press, 1994.

Thompson, Mabel, and the Historic Committee. *The Centenary Church: The United Church of Canada. 24 Main Street West, Hamilton, Ontario. The Church in the Heart of Hamilton since 1868.* Hamilton, ON. Booklet [n.d.].

Turcotte, Dorothy, and Grimsby Historical Archives. *Coaster Enthusiast of Canada: Closed Canadian Parks.* Online: http://cec.chebucto.org/ClosPark/Grimsby.html (accessed summer 2007).

Watson, Milton. *The Saga of a City: 300 Years of Progress in Hamilton*. Hamilton: Hamilton Spectator, 1938. Reprinted 1947.

Woods, Bruce A. "The Great Revival of 1857." *Arise Magazine*, Fall 1988, 32–35.

———. "The Great Hamilton Revival of 1857." Handout Essay for the Christian Business Men's Luncheon, Stanley Avenue Baptist Church, Hamilton, Ontario, n.d.

Younans, Harriet Phelps. *Grimsby Park Historical and Geographical Sketches*. Grimsby, ON, 1900.

General Index

Scripture Index

www.ingramcontent.com/pod-product-compliance
Lightning Source LLC
Chambersburg PA
CBHW071401160426
42812CB00085B/1073